CO-HUMAN HARMONY

Using Our Shared Humanity to Bridge Divides

Rev. Gudjon Bergmann

Harmony Interfaith Initiative
www.harmonyii.org

Published by Harmony Interfaith Initiative
and Flaming Leaf Press

ISBN: 978-0-9973012-5-0

*"Harmony makes small things grow,
lack of it makes great things decay."*

Sallust

CONTENTS

ACKNOWLEDGMENTS

My wife, Johanna Boel Bergmann, is my supporter in chief. She gives me inspiration, editing assistance, and provides for our family while I write. Without her, this book would never have seen the light of day. She has my eternal gratitude for that and so much more.

I also appreciate the assistance I got from my mother, Gudrun Bergmann, and my stepdaughter, Bara Steinunn Jonasdottir, who helped me by providing feedback and valuable insights.

The nineteen contributors, who took the time to answer the three questions I sent them without receiving any compensation, have my sincere thanks. Their perspectives added much value to this book.

The organizations that I mention on the following pages, especially iACT (Interfaith Action of Central Texas) and Dialogue Institute Austin, have my admiration for the work that they do to promote harmony, peace, and justice.

Finally, and somewhat paradoxically, I am thankful to all those who have been increasing acrimony in society over the past few years. Their words and actions have brought much-needed attention to a growing problem and highlighted the need for work towards social harmony.

PRELUDE: WHAT TO EXPECT FROM THIS BOOK

Overview

- Gathered and developed for the purpose of creating social harmony
- Provides simplified but undiluted guidelines
- A variety of contributors add perspectives
- Chapters are structured for maximum readability
- Adopt what resonates with you and leave the rest

The material in this book was gathered and developed for one purpose, to increase social harmony. The principles we live by at Harmony Interfaith Initiative—from our choice to pursue progress rather than perfection, choose strategies over platitudes, continually learn and grow, and work towards harmony rather than uniformity—

are all reflected on the following pages. Our all-inclusive definition of faith, as the *complete trust, confidence or strong belief in someone or something*, means that we do not merely seek to create better relations between people of different faiths but also between people of strong opposing beliefs. To us, interfaith means the continual improvement of interrelations between people who have different worldviews.

Simplified and Undiluted

Over the years, I have repeatedly been told that I have a knack for simplifying complex ideas without diluting them. That is what I have attempted to do throughout this book. I cite a variety of sources for corroboration and give subjective examples—both from my own life and the lives of workshop participants—but my primary goal is to offer down-to-earth, easy-to-read, undiluted guidelines based on relevant information.

That said, the book is a reflection of my preferences and is presented through the prism of my character and writing style.

To provide diversity of thought, I have included input from a variety of other people in an addendum titled, *Variations: What Bridge-Builders Say About Harmony*.

Structured for Readability

Being an avid reader myself, I usually devour somewhere between a book a week to a book a month. My reasons for reading differ. Sometimes I just want the essential information and the author can't get to the point quickly enough. Other times I savor the stories and fixate on the details.

I have tried to accommodate both needs in this book. If you only want the main points, you will benefit from subheadings and clearly marked passages, plus an overview at the start of every chapter. If you want stories and personal details, there are plenty of those to go around as well.

I encourage you to take notes as you read. Your ideas and insights may become more valuable to your efforts than anything I have written.

I also urge you to complete the suggested activities in the *personal initiative sections* after each chapter. Reading stimulates thought, but action changes lives.

Having a Conversation

Throughout, I invite you to imagine that we're having a conversation. Even though my words are presented in monologue format, your inner responses will convert them into a form of dialogue.

I ask a question and you respond internally, I make an argument and you counter it, I tell a story that reminds you of another story… and so it goes on and on.

If you find yourself enjoying the dialogue, you can make our conversation fully interactive by sending me an email at *revbergmann@harmonyii.org* or chatting with me on our social media channels.

Adopt What Resonates With You

Now, if something I have written rubs you the wrong way—and it probably will since the topic is sensitive and I am offering personal insights—you have three options. You can (1) throw the book away, (2) look past the idea or (3) try to figure out why it triggered you.

In my early twenties, I was halfway done with a book by M. Scott Peck when I became so offended by something he wrote about religion that I threw the book away. Several years later, I finished reading it and aside from that one thing, which I still found somewhat offensive, it was a great book. In fact, I have used many of the practical ideas I learned from it since.

There have been other times when I have gained exceptional insights from pausing and looking at why something triggered me. The Swiss psychiatrist and psychoanalyst, Carl Jung, used to say that everything that irritates us about others is something we should look at in ourselves. There is value in reflection.

Accordingly, you don't have to like or accept all the ideas that I present. Simply adopt what resonates with you and leave the rest.

You Have My Appreciation

It's easy to become jaded in the modern atmosphere of division. I want to thank you for taking the time to read this book and for showing interest in social harmony. We need more people like you who are willing to look for solutions and work towards their implementation. Please know that I have done everything in my power to make it worth your while.

Harmoniously,

Rev. Gudjon Bergmann
Harmony Interfaith Initiative
www.harmonyii.org

OVERTURE: WHY PEOPLE SEEK HARMONY

Overview

- People seek harmony due to varying degrees of acrimony
- Human beings are naturally inclined to choose peaceful relations
- In democracies around the world, citizens are responsible for maintaining harmony in their communities
- Harmony exists on a spectrum and progress needs to be celebrated
- We, the willing, need to have a vision for the future, accompanied with modest and measurable short-term goals

Why do people seek harmony? The answer to that question is simple. People seek harmony because they experience acrimony and discord.

They may be prompted by slight discomfort or faced with an overbearing dissonance, but, on average, people do not seek harmony until they experience some type of friction. When life vibrates at a harmonious frequency there is no need to seek something better. It's only when the rhythm of life is disrupted that people pay attention.

The obvious follow-up question is: How much discomfort are people willing to suffer before they seek change? It differs. Some people have trained themselves to live in a continual state of harmony and the slightest disturbance will prompt them to recalibrate. Others have either knowingly or unknowingly numbed or hardened themselves to the forces of discord so that nothing short of a catastrophe will get their attention.

An ancient parable tells us that some people are like attentive horses that move quickly when they see the shadow of a whip, while others are like stubborn horses that need to be whipped every step of the way.

If This Continues...

As a writer, most of my thinking happens when I am away from my computer, usually while I am walking. There is something about walking that stimulates my mind and helps me see things from different perspectives.

In 2017, I went on one of my contemplative walks. On this particular fall day, division was on my mind. I was reflecting on the outrage and anger that seemed so pervasive on social media;

the street violence that I had witnessed with increasing frequency in the news; the friendships and romantic relationships I had seen splinter because of differing ideologies; the strained family gatherings I had attended in recent years; the feelings of dread and fear that had been conveyed to me by Muslim friends in the interfaith community; the race-related rhetoric that was getting more toxic and contentious every day; and the anti-religious sentiment that was growing louder among many of my nonreligious friends.

All of this division was affecting me, creating feelings of irritation, anger, and frustration.

As I walked around my neighborhood, along pastel-colored houses with white picket fences, I reflected on the social fissures that were opening underneath the surface. Images, words, and emotions trundled through my head.

On every issue, on every front, it felt like discord was growing. People on all sides seemed to be becoming more convinced of the righteousness of their cause. Compromise had become a four-letter word and otherizing seemed to be the order of the day.

'What if this continues,' I thought to myself. 'What if the forces of division become stronger and stronger every year? Where will it end in five, ten, or fifteen years?'

I allowed my imagination to carry me into the future as I considered the answers.

What I saw in my mind's eye wasn't pretty.

From the Bottom Up!

'Something has to be done!'

That was my thinking when I returned from my walk. In an effort to be positive, I reminded myself that some of the best solutions have come from people who've allowed themselves to be temporarily pessimistic, who've envisioned the worst possible outcomes and then worked tirelessly to make sure they didn't materialize.

But my attempts to be positive did not last long that day. Self-doubt took over. 'Who do I think I am? What do I think I can accomplish? This is a large-scale problem. I am just one man with no following, no economic power, and no political leverage. What can I possibly do to harmonize the social discord that seems to be affecting everyone, not only in my adopted country (the USA) but also in my birth country (Iceland) and all around the world?'

As we will discuss later in the book, self-doubt can be a powerful detractor. It has kept many people from doing what they can. It almost stopped me dead in my tracks.

Thankfully, I stumbled on the following quote from Nobel Peace Prize laureate Betty Williams:

"Turmoil is everywhere, and the whole world is waiting for solutions to come from the top down. That's not how it works – community change from the bottom up makes a real difference."

From the bottom up. Those words caught my attention. Waiting for the federal government, my state government, local city council, or even well-meaning organizations to solve any of this wasn't likely to bear fruit… but I could work from the bottom up.

I could use my talents for teaching and writing to have an impact. I could throw my stone in the pond and hope it would create ripples. I could do something.

Beyond Wishful Thinking

As I looked around for solutions, one thing became clear to me. Telling people to "be nice" or "be friends" or even to "live by the Golden Rule" wasn't going to be enough in this atmosphere of discord. If I were to have an influence, I would need to move beyond wishful thinking, forsake platitudes, and discard clichés. I would need actual strategies and ideas that have worked to advance social harmony and communal bridge-building around the world.

I went to work, reading and researching for weeks on end. Correspondingly, I sorted through my accumulated arsenal of wisdom in search of solutions. Once I had gathered enough relevant information and practical tactics — all included in this book — I began disseminating the material.

The first opportunity to do so dropped into my lap. Shortly before Thanksgiving in 2017, Simone Talma Flowers, the executive director at iACT (Interfaith Action of Central Texas), asked me to write a column for the Austin American-Statesman. The article was better received than I had dared to hope. I got emails and phone calls from people I didn't know—which any writer knows is rare—all telling me how my thoughts on social harmony resonated with them.

Using that minor success as a stepping-stone, I reached out and was invited to speak at several Christian churches, a Buddhist temple, and a gathering of New Age thinkers in early 2018. Parallel to that, I increased my participation in local interfaith events.

In early February of the same year, I decided to take my efforts a step further and created my own organization called Harmony Interfaith Initiative. That spring I partnered with Charter for Compassion to offer an international online course that drew nearly three hundred participants from over twenty-five countries. I expanded my network to include people from a variety of bridge-building organizations across the country. To top it all off, I wrote this book.

The project started with a walk and has turned into something more. I am still in the early stages, but reverberations of what little I have done are already being felt farther away than I could have anticipated.

By telling you my story, I hope to encourage you to do what you can, with what you have, where you are. That is all I have done and will continue to do.

Can Harmony Be Achieved?

Let's back up a moment and ask a few questions that must be on your mind, just like they were on mine, questions like:

- Is harmony even possible?
- Can it ever be achieved on a communal level?
- Isn't man condemned to live in a state of constant strife and struggle?
- Is there any example in history of social harmony on a large scale?

These are all are reasonable questions. For answers, let me defer to someone much wiser than myself. Here are the words of Gandhi taken from his book, *Non-Violent Resistance (Satyagraha)*:

"*History, as we know it, is a record of the wars of the world, and so there is a proverb among Englishmen that a nation which has no history, that is, no wars, is a happy nation. How kings played, how they became the enemies of one another, how they murdered one another, is found accurately recorded in history, and if this were all that had happened in the world, it would have ended long ago. If the story of the universe had commenced with wars, not a man would have been found alive today [...] The fact that there are so many men still alive in the world shows that it is based not on the force of arms but on the force of truth or love. Therefore, the greatest and most unimpeachable evidence of the success of this force is to be found in the fact that, in spite of the wars of the world, it still lives on. [...]*

Little quarrels of millions of families in their daily lives disappear before the exercise of this force. Hundreds of nations live in peace. History does not and cannot take note of this fact. History is really a record of every interruption of the even working of the force of love or of the soul. Two brothers quarrel; one of them repents and re-awakens the love that was lying dormant in him; the two again begin to live in peace; nobody takes note of this. But if the two brothers, through the intervention of solicitors or some other reason, take up arms or go to law – which is another form of the exhibition of brute force – their doing would be immediately noticed in the press, they would be the talk of their neighbors and would probably go down in history. And what is true of families and communities is true of nations. There is no reason to believe that there is one law for families and another for nations. History, then, is a record of an interruption of the course of nature. Soul-force, being natural, is not noted in history."

Gandhi made a strong argument in this passage. What he called soul-force (and I refer to as harmony) is the rule, not the exception. Modern news coverage reflects his theory. Only disruptive events are reported while the vast majority of people who go about their daily lives in peace are not deemed newsworthy.

Based on this reasoning, the good news, which is not being reported, is that harmony is a natural force. It has been sustained in some form in every society. As Gandhi pointed out, we would not be here today if it were the other way around.

There is a caveat to this way of viewing the world. While the need for harmony is in all of us, it does not become a central organizing principle in communities when people stand back and do nothing. In a civilized society, we humans are responsible for nurturing and sustaining the force of inter-relational harmony in our lives. Only by making it a priority can we achieve fewer disruptions and recalibrate relations when disturbances grow disproportionately, as they have in recent years.

The Democratic Dilemma

Democracies all around the globe are engaged in a grand experiment of self-governance. The balance is tricky. For the democratic process to work, all citizens must be committed to the peaceful transfer of power and to solving problems through dialogue and lawful behavior rather than coercion and violence.

On one end of the scales, people are committed to living harmoniously and in peace; on the other, they have vigorous debates about how to best run the government that they have chosen to serve them.

Compromise is a key element in this context. If a group of citizens decides, "it's our way or the highway," then the results are discontent and turmoil. Such unrest can lead to violent surges and that opens the door for rule through brute force. Historically, we've seen examples of this in dictatorships and during the rise of fascist governments, where social unrest has become so great that the people are no longer trusted to rule themselves. Benjamin Franklin aptly wrote that:

"Only a virtuous people are capable of freedom. As nations become corrupt and vicious, they have more need of masters."

Many scholars and statesmen have pointed out that the democratic and religious atmosphere

here in the USA is on the wrong track these days. The constant otherizing and dehumanizing is sowing seeds, fertilizing the ground for the possibility of physical violence or partial disen-franchisement of segments of the population—which, if we are being honest, has already occurred to a certain degree.

If we want to avoid the worst possible outcomes and stop acrimony from further spilling into the streets where it will cause greater social unrest, we need active groups of peacemakers, bridge-builders and harmonizers in every community. We must heed the words of Dr. Martin Luther King Jr. who said:

"Those who love peace must learn to organize as effectively as those who love war."

The Spectrum of Harmony

When my wife and I decided to name our organization Harmony Interfaith Initiative, we thought long and hard about what the word *harmony* would mean in the context of our work. The dictionary defines the term as *the quality of forming a pleasing and consistent whole*, but as we sought to deepen our understanding, we realized that the concept was more complicated than it appeared at first, especially because harmony exists on a spectrum.

In musical terms, a punk-rock garage band can sit on one end of the spectrum while the Vienna Boys Choir sits on the other. The reverberations from the choir may sound more pleasant, but we cannot deny the fact that the garage band is producing a version of musical harmony.

The same is true of social harmony. It exists on a spectrum from ceasing hostilities and tolerance to cooperation and fellowship. If people only accept the highest form of harmony, they will be unable to celebrate progress and that may accidentally stifle development altogether.

A simplified spectrum of harmony:

- Ceasing hostilities
- Tolerance
- Understanding
- Cooperation
- Friendship
- Fellowship
- Perfect harmony

Recently, several pundits and politicians from around the world have begun declaring that tolerance is no longer good enough; that we need to replace it with unconditional love and respect for each other.

While that is a beautiful sentiment (one we should surely strive towards), devaluing tolerance is not a step in the right direction. We can't cut the first few steps off a ladder and then ask people to follow us.

Tolerance is better than open hostilities. Tolerance suggests that even though we may disagree with each other, dislike each other's living arrangements, and disapprove of each other's beliefs, we are still tolerant and respect each other's freedom to choose our own paths so long as we do not cause harm to other people. In fact, sometimes tolerance is all we can hope for.

Take the example of a divorced couple. They are invited to a birthday party where everyone hopes they will hug it out and be friends, but the hosts utter a sigh of relief when the couple leaves the house without having made a scene. The divorcees may dislike each other but they tolerated each other's presence for the benefit of everyone else and that was enough. Maybe next time it will turn out better.

The reason why I am emphasizing the importance of tolerance is that human beings are not perfect, nor should we expect them to be. When we downplay tolerance, we have set the bar too high and most people will fail to meet our standards. We should instead celebrate progress every time a person moves in the direction of more social harmony because that brings all of us one step closer to friendship and fellowship.

More Complexity

In addition to existing on a spectrum, social harmony is *diverse*, as in, there are lots of different ways to achieve it (think of the near infinite varieties of music genres), it is *subjective*, as in, not everyone will like the same things (compare the likes and dislikes of a traditional New Yorker to those of a Texan, for example), and it is *relative*, because what seems out of place in one setting, fits perfectly in another.

Furthermore, disharmonies can contribute to harmony, just like a discordant jazz note may temporarily disturb the listener but once it is expressed and resolved, it contributes to the overall harmony.

Allowing for this variety, we can better appreciate the concept in social situations because harmony is often in the ear of the listener.

The Human Orchestra

Similes can be helpful teaching tools. By taking an abstract idea and comparing it to something literal and easy to understand a teacher can shorten the distance between confusion and comprehension.

I have found this to be true when I've likened humanity to an orchestra in my workshops. The comparison provides a fairly broad understanding of harmony. Thus, if we envision humanity as an orchestra—where we can either picture people as the instruments or the instruments as different world-views—we will probably want to do most, if not all, of the following:

a) Stop the Noise

The first step toward a harmonious melody is to stop the noise. If a select few incessantly bang their drums, scratch their strings, yammer loudly, or play their own fortissimo tunes without regards to their surroundings, the best intentions of the people around them will not matter. In the same way, if the human orchestra is to generate a harmonious melody, we must reduce violent actions and bombastic rhetoric, preferably through peaceful means. When things quiet down, there is a potential for something better to emerge.

b) Accept All Instruments

An orchestra only creates a limited variety of harmonies if everyone plays either the violin or the trumpet. Different instruments are needed to contrast and complement each other. In ancient Greece, woodworkers understood this. They joined together woods of opposing grains to create balance and harmony. The human race, with all its different cultures, theologies, and ideologies, has the potential to do the same.

In years past, people could get away with consorting only with those who shared their looks and ideologies, but in the modern era, where the sheer number of inhabitants is growing year by year and people are moving their cultures with them all around the globe, this is no longer a choice. Currently, two hundred and fifty million people are living outside their country of birth, and I am one of them. The human orchestra is stacked with a variety of instruments. Diversity is our reality. Accepting that is important.

c) Practice Our Instruments

If musicians don't practice, they are not able to play together. My friend used to be a middle school band director and he took great pleasure in seeing the progression from sixth grade to eighth grade; from the time when the kids entered band without knowing how to play to when they played together in more harmony. In that context, each culture, ideology, and theology on Earth has created an ideal of what a good person acts like.

In *The Varieties of Religious Experience*, William James pointed out that there is little difference between Stoic, Buddhist and Christian saints, that their lives are practically indistinguishable. His insight does not mean that there aren't any differences between those paths, rather that if each individual sincerely pursues and practices the best of what his or her culture, theology, and ideology has to offer, from agnostic humanists to the most pious Christians, then humanity will be better off as a whole, just like the orchestra is better off when individual players consistently practice their instruments. In the same way that innate musical talents need to be supplemented with practice, human seeds of goodness need to be nurtured to flourish.

d) Synchronize With Our Surroundings

An orchestra can only produce a captivating melody if all the players are in rhythm. Half of learning to play in an orchestra is about personal dedication; the other half is about synchronization. Synchronization is not the same as conformity. One approach values input from many different instruments towards a single melody while the other wants everyone to be the same. For the human orchestra to be harmonious, we must play our instruments to the best of our abilities and also synchronize with our surroundings.

As with every good simile, this one falls apart when we start to take it too literally. For example, it goes without saying that not everyone will be playing the same music and that, in a democracy, there will be no dictatorial conductor forcing everyone to follow the same rhythm—heck, some people will even refuse to play in the band.

Nevertheless, those limitations don't mean that the analogy can't be beneficial. With the right intent, we can begin by focusing on ourselves (our own instrument) and then synchronize with people in our surroundings (the orchestra), especially those who are also practicing (the willing). In the words of Sufi master Hazrat Inayat Khan:

"All the tragedy in the world, in the individual and in the multitude, comes from lack of harmony. And harmony is the best given by producing harmony in one's own life."

People who dismiss this notion as idealistic should consider the alternative. If people sit back, don't practice their instrument, won't even try to synchronize, and focus all their attention on creating brassy dissonance through divisive rhetoric and actions, then the human orchestra will keep on playing nonetheless, but the acrimonious discord will put the sound of nails scratching a blackboard to shame. In the long run, creating harmony will take hard work and the outcome probably won't be perfect. That's okay. It's better to be in a dedicated middle school band that hasn't quite gotten its act together than a hall full of musicians making disparate noises.

An Achievable Vision for the Future

The question we are faced with is a difficult one. How can we move this idea of harmony from the theoretical realm into our daily lives? From a realistic standpoint, we have to admit that human beings will never be in complete harmony with each other. Singing Kumbaya by the campfire is reserved for smaller groups, not the whole of humanity. There are just too many disparate views and competing interests for that to happen... but we can do better.

With that in mind, I've come up with what I believe to be an achievable vision for the future.

Here's my thinking.

According to sociologists, the average human being has the ability to truly connect with somewhere between 40-120 people. Within this core group are friends, co-workers, family members, and others that the person feels he or she can trust. We are not talking about the thousands of social media connections that some people have, rather the people that they turn to in times of need.

Now, imagine one or two willing and able bridge-builders within every such group, people who serve as mediators and peacemakers, who seek harmony rather than acrimony, and who are comfortable with being around others that don't believe or look as they do. Those one or two people could work openly towards harmony from within the group.

Visualize that. One or two people per group. That's all it takes to influence group dynamics.

A participant in one of my workshops presented me with the perfect musical analogy to illustrate my vision. She regularly joins a group of people who play Irish folk songs, and they seldom use sheet music. Because everyone is welcome to join this ensemble, participants either learn the tunes on their own or pick them up from each other. It's usually pretty chaotic.

The insertion of one or two outstanding musicians can have two effects. If the musicians try to show off, then the whole group suffers and people either withdraw or struggle to keep up. If, however, the musicians are patient and supportive of the group, then everyone plays better. One or two qualified people can have a ripple effect that is measurable on everything from rhythm to tone.

I firmly believe that skilled bridge-builders, who are committed to social harmony, can have similar effects on the core groups that they belong to—groups where trust is already established.

Furthermore, I believe that training one or two people per group is an achievable vision. In the short-term, we, the willing, can commit to being better bridge-builders ourselves while gently and lovingly supporting a new rhythm and a more harmonious tone for the people who are within our sphere of influence. In the long-term, we can train others who are willing to do the same. One or two people per group. That's all we need to make a real difference.

Making Harmony a Priority

As I mentioned earlier, our need for harmony

will be in direct relationship with the amount of acrimony we feel.

I recently spoke with a minister who was teaching in the outskirts of New York on 9/11 2001. He told me that he'd never seen strangers come together as they did in the weeks after the attack on the Twin Towers. People went out of their way to be nice to each other, support each other, smile at each other, and lend a helping hand wherever they could. He has not experienced anything like it since. In fact, he jokingly mentioned that an alien invasion might be the only way to bring humanity together in a similar fashion (which indecently was the plot in Kurt Vonnegut's book, *The Sirens of Titan*).

The truth is that work towards harmony often dissipates in rhythm with receding acrimony. People start to feel better and get sidetracked.

This is natural.

However, if you want to be a bridge-builder, you have to work against this instinctive urge. You have to make harmony important, either by continually reminding yourself of the worst that can happen or by envisioning the kind of world that you want to live in and work towards that every day.

Some days the carrot will be enough to spur you to action, other days only a vivid mental image of the stick will do the trick.

We Are Responsible

During our outreach efforts at Harmony Interfaith Initiative, we get a chance to talk to a variety of people and organizations. Some of those we contact point fingers and say: "It's not us. It's them. They started it. We are living in harmony with each other. They are the ones causing the ruckus."

That's often true.

It may be true in your case as well.

In fact, you may be doing your best to live in harmony and yet you cannot escape being disturbed by the drumbeat of discord around you. All of us have to face up to that reality. Life is not an elementary school playground. We can't wait for the teacher to come and make everything better, even if 'they' started it.

We are responsible.

Even if we did not create the acrimony, even if we weren't the ones who created the divide, we can be bridge-builders, healers, harmonizers, and a vital part of the solution.

We can reach out across divides that we did not create for the sake of social harmony. We can cause positive reverberations to offset negative discord. We can be the change we want to see in the world.

* * *

PERSONAL INITIATIVES

Status Check

Answering the following questions in writing will clarify your current position. In the same way that you need to know your location before you plot a new course on a map, it can be helpful to know where you stand in relation to social harmony before you attempt to make improvements.

1. How do you define harmony?
2. Why do you think it is important to work towards harmony?
3. What kind of divisions do you see in our society that you want to bridge?
4. What triggers you about other people's behavior?
5. Do you spend any time with people who have different ideologies than you do (religious, spiritual, political, nutritional, success, etc.)? If yes, how do those interactions usually go (i.e., where do they land on the spectrum of harmony)?
6. Compare yourself with other people in your circle of awareness:
    a. What do you have in common?
    b. What are the differences?
7. Do you follow any guidelines when you enter into a dialogue with other people? If yes, what are they?
8. Is there an area in your life in which you would call yourself a true believer (that is, where you have a very strong attraction to ideas/lifestyles/rules etc.)?
9. If harmony is to be reached within our society:
    a. Do you have to change?
    b. Do other people have to change?
10. Is it easy or hard for you to change your beliefs, thoughts, emotions, and actions?

11. What are your goals for the ideas and strategies you will find in this book?
12. What stood out to you about your answers?

Once you are done reading this book, you may want to revisit these questions and answer them again to see if your answers have changed.

Two Lists for Reflection

The following two lists demonstrate the most common reasons why people come to my lectures and workshops. One list reveals an *aversion to acrimony*, where pain and displeasure are the driving forces behind people's decisions to attend. The other list describes *constructive intentions*, where attendees want to do something to counter the forces of division and are looking for solutions. These are reasons given by actual participants. I urge you to take a moment and read through them. Reflect on your motives for reading this book while you explore other people's aversions and aspirations.

Aversion to Acrimony

- "I am painfully aware of the cost of disharmony in my personal life, my relationships, and in the world."
- "I stopped interacting with people due to differences in religious ideology."
- "I visited Jerusalem and was dismayed by the enmity between Jewish and Muslim residents there."

- "There is such a divide in the US politically right now. My friends and family appear to want the same things, peace and happiness, yet they have totally different political beliefs. I find myself unable to communicate with them."
- "I am disheartened by the lack of civility and dehumanizing rhetoric these days."
- "Friends who I've known for twenty years are suddenly strangers whom I can't talk to… our differences a gulf between us."
- "These are dark times. There are so many areas of conflict between countries, religions, genders, cultures, generations, and political ideologies."
- "I am always looking for the final strike, the last shoe to drop. I am tired of crying."
- "I am a Christian minister and the divisive rhetoric within the 'camps' of Christianity belies the message we are to promote. I need to do a better job of affirming my beliefs without dismissing, demeaning or discounting others."
- "I am exhausted."
- "As a social worker, I tried to be compassionate and understanding. Now that I have retired, I sometimes allow myself the easy way out and just look at what is wrong with the other person's point of view."
- "I have concerns about the rising levels of rancor in public discourse and my own increasing anxiety about it all."

Seeking Solutions

- "I am engaged in a mission to reduce poverty, organize educational opportunities, and create positive practices. I am intrigued by the interreligious approach."
- "I want to uncover strategies to celebrate differences both in my academic work and in my life."
- "I am looking for tools for building harmonious relationships within diverse communities."
- "I have an active interest in interfaith dialogue and harmony."
- "I want to gain skills to communicate effectively and compassionately."
- "I will be a better citizen and teacher if I learn strategies for building bridges."
- "I want to learn practical ways to communicate with people that I disagree with without compromising my values or losing myself."
- "I want to be reminded of the fact that people are fundamentally kind."
- "I am participating to be more comfortable with asking good questions, to increase my listening skills, and be more able to respond with compassion—a little at a time."
- "I am nudging myself back to a more compassionate perspective."
- "I am a professor of politics and am looking for ideas to add to my

curriculum."

- "I have decided to initiate a bridge-building program in my apartment building and am looking for tools."
- "I want to generate fertile ground for my granddaughter and future generations."
- "As a teacher of religious studies, I am really interested in exploring the positive impact of interfaith work with my students."

MOVEMENT 1: RECOGNIZE THE SIGNIFICANCE OF CO-HUMANITY

Overview

- Each human being is comprised of two personas
- The ideological persona includes beliefs and values
- The human persona reflects shared humanity
- Two extremes are dehumanization and a refusal to discuss differences
- In the current atmosphere, we have erred on the side of the ideological persona and need to recognize the significance of our co-humanity

It was June 18, the day after my ordination in 2017. I had spent the preceding week in upstate New York with a wonderful group of mentors and fellow students. Our ordination ceremony took place on June 17 in an old church in Manhattan and I was returning home to Texas an ordained Interfaith Minister—a role I define as someone who has studied the world's religions, resonated with their core ideals and has no objections to serving all of them in some way.

The New Jersey air terminal was busy, teeming with people returning home from their weekend activities. I found a vacant seat and ate my breakfast. As I chewed on my tuna sandwich, I turned my gaze to one of the terminal TVs where Fareed Zakaria was doing his Sunday show on CNN. There were a number of people on his panel talking about the topic of gun violence and terrorism, including Padraig O'Malley, a man who had been instrumental in the Northern Ireland peace process.

When it was his turn, O'Malley pointed out that we all have two personas, the human and the ideological, and that the only way to dehumanize someone is to start seeing him or her as an ideologue only. Furthermore, he said that an overemphasis on ideological differences could diminish our shared humanity and create a vacuum for violence.

Subconscious Digestion

Despite what you may think, this was not a light bulb moment for me. I didn't exclaim *Eureka* and jump out of my chair. All I remember doing is nodding my head and thinking to myself, 'Hmm… the human and ideological personas… that's interesting.' Nonetheless, it appears that my subconscious mind took the idea more seriously and went to work on it.

Why do I say that?

Because the idea kept popping up as I watched the world around me for the next few months. In the hidden recesses of my mind, something took the idea and chewed on it like a dog on a bone, refusing to let it go, comparing it to all the information about religion, politics, spirituality, and psychology that I'd gathered in my lifetime. Every time the idea surfaced in my conscious mind, it felt more refined than the last time, yet I had not spent any time consciously mulling it over or investigating it.

Accordingly, when I began seeking solutions to social discord, the idea of the two personas planted itself front and center in my awareness. Since then it has been a guiding light in my efforts and I have made a conscious effort to understand it from as many sides as possible. The following reflects my current understanding.

The Ideological Persona

The ideological persona consists of beliefs and values, including ideas, stories, and principles, that people have chosen, through reason, emotion or repetition, to put faith in even though there is little empirical evidence to either prove or disprove their validity.

The distinguishing feature is *belief*.

Most ideologies cannot be independently proven or disproven, which is why arguments can be made for or against almost any conceptual stance and people can be swayed with ideological rhetoric.

The ideological persona plays an important role in our lives. It develops with more consistency during adolescence, as our likes and dislikes become clearer, and matures into a central part of our character as we age. Beliefs and values provide us with a moral compass, an identity, connections to groups of likeminded people and a sense of purpose, to name a few.

To summarize, the ideological persona makes up our personal philosophy and produces the color of the glasses through which we view and interpret life. It incorporates all types of ideologies, including:

- Politics: How we believe society should be run
- Religion and spirituality: What we believe to be of utmost importance
- Morality: How we believe we should behave and treat each other
- Success: What it means to be successful
- Nutrition: What we should eat — which is currently a blend of evidence and ideology
- …and much more

Once ideologies have been further developed, categorized, and are being consistently utilized, they become –isms, such as:

- Capitalism
- Creationism
- Egalitarianism
- Environmentalism

- Existentialism
- Fascism
- Feminism
- Fundamentalism
- Humanism
- Imperialism
- Impressionism
- Isolationism
- Legalism
- Militarism
- Pacifism
- Pantheism
- Polytheism
- Racism
- Realism
- Romanticism
- Scholasticism
- Skepticism
- Socialism
- Surrealism
- Totalitarianism
- Utilitarianism
- ...et cetera... (there is no shortage of –isms)

In a perfect world, people would preface their belief and value statements with sentences like:

"I believe..."
"What I think..."
"I value..."
"I prefer..."
"My view is..."

...and so on, but ideologies often become so ingrained that they fuse with empirical facts and people stop seeing them for what they are, namely, beliefs and values. Instead, people present their ideologies as factual statements, saying things like "this is the way things *are*" or "this is *the only truth.*" Getting people to acknowledge that their beliefs and values are, in fact, beliefs and values is often an important step in the direction of lessening tensions and bridging divides.

It goes without saying that not everyone shares the same ideologies, beliefs or values, especially in a diverse society, which means that the ideological persona provides us with both opportunities and obstacles.

Ideological persona = Beliefs and values that cannot be independently proven or disproven

The Human Persona

The human persona consists of elements that are shared by every other human being on the planet. Maslow's hierarchy of needs is a good place to start when we are trying to understand co-humanity. The model is usually presented in a pyramid format, with basic needs at the bottom and self-actualization needs at the top.

Similarities abound when we look at the basics. Every human being has physiological needs for food, shelter, water, warmth, and rest, and has safety needs, including requirements for security, a steady job or income, and more. Most of us fulfill these rudimentary needs in similar ways.

Our paths diverge a bit when it comes to belongingness needs, including intimate relationships and friendships, and esteem needs, since the variety of ways in which they can be satisfied is greater. Still, because the first four needs are so-called deficiency needs—meaning that human beings usually pursue them until they are met—most everyone resonates with other human beings and understands why they are doing what they are doing when they are attempting to satisfy the four basic needs.

When it comes to self-actualization needs, people are vastly different in their approaches and ideologies, which means that there is less parity to be found by comparing them.

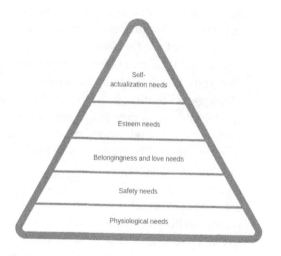

The lower the needs are in the pyramid and the more fundamental they are to our existence, the easier it is to connect through them. In fact, making a connection with another human persona can often feel instinctual at the basic level because we share more elements with less diversity. Let me give you a few examples:

a) A generous host can easily connect with the human persona in his guests by (1) offering food, water, warmth and rest, (2) attending to safety and security if required, (3) offering friendship, and (4) making them feel worthwhile.

b) Human-to-human connections are frequently on full display during natural disasters. People set aside ideological differences and do their best to help fellow human beings that they do not know. There are no screener questions to check for ideological purity, only a shared sense of compassion because everyone's needs at that moment are the same.

c) Many find it easy to relate to babies because they have not yet developed a robust ideological identity (incidentally, the same can be said about pets since they share basic survival needs and some emotional components but have no well-defined ideological persona).

d) As an example of the opposite, people are often disappointed when athletes and actors — with whom they have shared strong co-human empathy — express ideological views that are different from their own because the sense of shared humanity feels somehow diminished.

Making co-human connections becomes more difficult as complexity increases. Once we get to emotional needs, for instance, a wide range of human emotions can make it challenging for people to relate to each other.

Interestingly enough, the lowest common denominator within the emotional domain is not happiness (even though offering a smile rarely fails) but rather *suffering*. Since everyone feels miserable at one point or another in his or her life, pain can serve as a mega-connector for human beings in the right circumstances.

The evidence of friendships and support groups around the world clearly shows this. If I am vulnerable enough to share my pain with you and you have experienced something similar (or can imagine my pain), then we have made an instant co-human connection. The poet, Henry Wadsworth Longfellow, rightly observed that:

"If we could read the secret history of our enemies, we should find in each man's life sorrow and suffering enough to disarm all hostility."

Studying human needs can give insights into the essential elements that constitute the human persona, but that's only the beginning. I encourage you to strengthen your understanding of co-humanity with personal observations and to explore several other psycho-spiritual, sociological, behavioral, and anthropological models.

To see the human persona clearly, look for things that *we all share*, regardless of ideological differences.

Human persona = Universally shared human elements

Social Harmony and the Two Personas

The concept of social harmony originates in both personas. In the human persona, longing for harmonious relations arises naturally because of the need for belongingness and love. We all yearn for it in our own way. At the same time, social harmony is an ideology that some people believe in while others oppose it with the belief that might is right and that humans are destined to be in a violent struggle for dominance.

In the marketplace of ideas, those who prefer harmonious relations need to be willing to defend their approach in a nonviolent way and gently persuade others to do the same. To paraphrase Dr. King from earlier in the book, 'those who love harmony must learn to organize as effectively as those who love acrimony.'

Thankfully, the case for harmony is made stronger because it is based on a built-in emotional need and therefore brings together both personas.

Two Extremes

As far as I can tell, there are two extremes related to this idea of the two personas.

One extreme is the danger of *dehumanization*, as O'Malley pointed out in the TV interview I referred to earlier. When people focus on ideological differences and consistently refer to each other using discriminating labels then a door is opened to alienating 'the other' and making the human being somehow less than human. That creates justifications to deny basic human needs, a willingness to go along with social marginalization, and a readiness to condone violence. Once violence is condoned, the otherizing is complete.

The other extreme claims that *"we are all the same"* and misinterprets any attempt to discuss differing beliefs as an attack on someone's humanity. Ideological differences are dismissed as trivial and only the human persona is allowed to exist. This kind of reductionism can cause problems, but people who refuse to see ideological differences usually do not resort to violence.

We Have Created a Social Imbalance

From an integral standpoint, every human being is a complex mix of these two personas, but our information-driven society has placed such an overemphasis on the ideological persona that it has created an imbalance, politicizing and polarizing everything in ideological terms, from word-use to basic human characteristics such as gender and skin color.

Based on this discrepancy, I can say without hesitation that the most important project at this moment in history is to reclaim a social connection to the human persona, to move away from dehumanizing and otherizing in the direction of co-humanizing. Let me give you a few examples to support my hypothesis.

The Dangers of Otherizing

"These people. What *these people* don't understand is..."

That's how it often starts. Otherizing begins innocently enough, but before we know it we're stuck on a slippery slope to extremism. Attempts to create a little bit of an ideological distance often end in full-blown labeling where no co-humanity is allowed.

As such, most labeling starts out generically. In the political realm, it begins with something mundane like liberal or conservative, but can then devolve quickly into something much nastier like baby-killer and gun-nut. Obviously, labeling is not restricted to politics and the escalation can be intense. As divides grow, Muslims become towel-heads and terrorists, Christians become gay-haters and hypocrites, poor people become losers and takers, believers become religious-nuts and zealots, atheists become the spawns of Satan... and on it goes.

The more extreme the labels become, the easier it is to stop seeing 'the other' as fully human. Betty Williams underscores this point forcefully:

"It is much harder to kill your near neighbor than the thousands of unknown and hostile aliens at the other end of a nuclear missile. We have to create a world in which there are no unknown, hostile aliens at the other end of any missiles."

With the overuse of ideological rhetoric, people have created aliens in their own backyards, failing to see that their neighbor is equally human. How can people love their neighbor as themselves if they cannot see their own humanity reflected in their neighbor?

Lack of Nuance

The social sciences have shown time and time again that people's beliefs are generally more nuanced than they appear to be. Believers in a particular cause or ideology may have core values in common with their group, but, when they get a chance to illustrate their personal preferences in detail most of them employ a sliding scale with some variations.

For most of us, knowing that serves as a welcome relief. People are not homogenous; their beliefs are more varied than they appear to be.

Unfortunately, this reality can be easily overlooked from a distance. From the opposite side of a socially created chasm, the view is often black and white with no room for shades of gray. Anyone who slightly associates with a specific worldview is perceived as believing the most extreme version of that ideology. Such an inaccurate perception creates cognitive dissonance. What is true about most of us—in essence, that our beliefs and values exist in shades of gray, that we are not extremists—is not true about the other side, or, at least, that is what we may think.

The problem is that without having direct conversations, we cannot ascertain for ourselves whether beliefs are nuanced or if people are as fanatical as we imagine them to be. For the sake of social harmony, we need to be willing to explore the possibility of finding nuance for three reasons:

1. Nuanced beliefs are the de facto human mindset

2. If people are treated like extremists, they can rise to the occasion
3. People, who are not extremists, can start to see others who employ extremist labels indiscriminately as extremists themselves, leaving no room for bridge-building or compromise

This last point is probably the most important one. For instance, if Claire is not an extremist, but is frequently called one despite her nuanced beliefs, she will start to see those who use unjust labels about her as extremists themselves and will not want to engage with them in any way, thusly widening an already growing divide.

Refusal to Engage in Dialogue

As we will explore in greater detail later in the book, honest and respectful dialogue is a vital part of generating social harmony, but, for that to take place, people must at a minimum be capable of seeing each other as co-human. No one will ever be persuaded by a convincing argument if they are not first respected as human beings. The peacemaker, O'Malley, explains this concept in his book about the Israeli-Palestinian conflict:

"The important component is respect; respect is more embracive than trust. Until each side reaches a level of understanding of the other's narrative that facilitates a willingness to accord parity of esteem, peace agreements will likely falter..."

In a world where people see only ideological differences, where contempt of 'the other' has become all too common, then why on earth would anyone want to enter into a dialogue with someone who they feel is not equally human and therefore has no right to their personal narrative? There is no room for dialogue in such an atmosphere.

Widening the Divide

Polarized media plays a substantial role in expanding divides. Consumers now choose media outlets that serve 'news of the day' in narratives that fit their worldview. Confirmation bias has become big business.

Nowhere, however, is the gap widening faster and in a more pronounced way than on social media. There is a simple reason for that.

Think about it. Of the two personas, which one do you interact more with on social media?

Exactly — it's the ideological persona.

In fact, nowhere is the ideological persona more noticeable and less nuanced than on social media. Everything is black and white. You are either for or against. Shared memes and bite-size snippets work like dynamite to enlarge divides between people.

Constant ideological sharing is creating more and more personal distance — even between people who've known and liked each other for a long time. "How can such and such believe that?" is one of the main complaints that I hear in my workshops.

Road Rage and Internet Rage

John Cleese created a fabulous miniseries for BBC 1 in 2001 called *The Human Face*. In the series, he presented a segment about road rage that I have often used to illustrate Internet rage.

Cleese and his team demonstrated that when two people are walking down the street and bump into each other, there is usually a slight exchange of facial expressions and body language that diffuses tension and allows both people to continue on their way without incident. When people are in their cars, however, there are no such exchanges. Without diffusing facial interactions, emotions can flare up and end in absolute fury. That is road rage.

I believe that the same is true about the Internet. In the online domain, there are no face-to-face interactions, no exchanges of body language, and little or no nuance in communications. People can spin themselves into states of outrage in reaction to what they perceive as personal slights, reacting to an imagined tone and body language that often reflects their own emotional state more than anything else.

Would things be different if these people were in each other's presence?

The answer is most likely yes. At least two things would be altered. One, general social conduct would prevent one person from saying what he or she wrote without any hesitation on the Internet. Two, if the person said something inappropriate, the face-to-face interaction might well diffuse the situation.

There is an exception to this reasoning in our changing world. Because people are relentlessly exposed to ideological differences, both in traditional media and on social media, in-person interactions may no longer be enough to diffuse situations like they used to be.

For example, everyone in the USA is familiar with the idea of being exposed to differing political views during Thanksgiving celebrations. Before the Internet, Uncle Bob might have said something inappropriate or politically insensitive, but because Samara had known him as a nice human being for most of her life, she would have shrugged it off. Nowadays, she would have been exposed Uncle Bob's rants and inappropriate memes on social media every day for a year, and when she finally met him at Thanksgiving, she'd have a hard time seeing him as a nice human being. She might, in fact, be unable to shrug it off and enjoy his company.

What is true about Uncle Bob is also true about every other assertive meme-sharer and ideologue. This is one of the challenges of our times, one that we must tackle if we want to live in harmony with each other. We are on each other's social media feeds all the time, but not in each other's lives.

Online Ideological Tribes

To further complicate things, we now live in an era where online ideological tribes are growing in number and diversity, where everything from large groups to small fringe camps can easily congregate because geographical restrictions have been eliminated thanks to the Internet.

If you think of how tribes were traditionally formed, entry barriers used to be a mix of family, friendships, geography, interests, strong beliefs, trustworthiness and more. Today, ideological purity is the only measurement that counts. If you doubt me, try entering an ideological space online and say something remotely antithetical to the beliefs that the group shares. You will get clobbered. When ideological purity is the only thing that binds the group together, even modest critiques and friendly evaluations are met with harsh reactions.

As in previous examples, the missing element in these online tribes is the human persona. There are no face-to-face interactions and no body language to interpret. Thousands of years of collective evolution, from tone, tenor, eye contact, energy, micro-expressions, and non-threatening demeanor are all absent, which means that we are navigating in uncharted territory.

Recognizing Co-Humanity in Others

Will everything change for the better when we find ways to incorporate the human persona in our interactions?

It may not be that simple, but overall, the answer is yes. I believe that we must find as many ways as possible to incorporate the human persona into our lives by increasing human-to-human contact, reminding ourselves that at the end of our keyboard is a person with a beating heart who feels and breathes and loves and suffers, and by supplementing every statement about ideological differences with a sense of shared humanity. In the words of Archbishop Desmond Tutu:

"All of our humanity is dependent upon recognizing the humanity in others."

We can only create harmony and build bridges between strong differing beliefs if co-humanity is the link that ties us together.

The Dark Side of Humanity

In historical context, focusing on our shared humanity hasn't always had a positive undertone. The other side of our unique potential for love, compassion, tolerance, forgiveness, and empathy (all seeds that need to be nurtured) is that human beings have a history of being the most overtly sexual, aggressive, destructive, and possessive animals on the planet. We are a strange mix of dust and divinity.

Granted, struggling with our dark side sometimes gives rise to positive elements, such as forgiveness and empathy (as the term *'we are only human'* suggests) but don't be surprised if you get a negative response when you ask someone to focus on shared humanity. They may be thinking of all the bad stuff that is uniquely human, not all the good stuff.

I mention this to provide a balanced view of the term. Awareness of the dark side—including the animal instincts that reside within each of us and the psychological shadow (as Jung termed it) that lurks beneath the surface — can be beneficial.

Nevertheless, in light of our communal longing for harmony, I ask you to place more focus on our *shared needs*, as described by Maslow, and our *potential for goodness and growth*. When you focus on those aspects, you may get others to do the same.

Do We All Want the Same Things?

Several years ago, I witnessed an argument on television that centered on the Middle East — a contentious topic to say the least. The interviewee had spent several years in Afghanistan, Pakistan, and Lebanon.

She was giving her insights into daily life there when the interviewer asked: "What was the one thing that you took away from your experience?" She replied: "That we all want the same things." To which he replied: "No, we don't. No… we don't!!!"

The interviewer then angrily recounted all the ways in which the liberal West and the Middle East are different, how our values and beliefs collide and so on.

She tried to get a word in edgewise to explain what she meant, in essence, that we all want the same things for our children, that we all want safety, security, shelter, access to sustenance, and emotional connections, but he wouldn't listen. The interview, which had been amicable up until that point, never recovered.

In the context of this chapter about the two personas, we can easily see where the quarrel originated. She was talking about the human persona while he was talking about the ideological persona. Human personas across the world want the same things, including food, shelter, warmth, security, love, family, friendships, etc. Ideological personas do not. That is the crux of the matter.

Human Bonds and Ideological Diversity

Having the two personas in our vocabulary provides us with a way to address these differences without reducing one to the other. We can use our shared humanity to create strong bonds, tend to each other's basic needs, and affirm that we all belong to the human tribe. Concurrently, we need to allow for ideological diversity and maintain the ability to discuss ideological differences without hypersensitivity, name-calling, or violence. Only by using such a balanced approach, being simultaneously diverse and connected, just like an orchestra, can we generate co-human harmony.

* * *

PERSONAL INITIATIVES

List Co-Human Elements

Make a list of the elements that you share with every other human being on this planet. Write everything that comes to mind and then add to your list every time you encounter something new that is distinctly human.

Having such a catalog will accomplish two things. First, you will be searching for everything that you have in common with people you encounter. Second, an ongoing and ever-growing list will strengthen the bonds you feel with the rest of humanity. It will remind you that even though we may belong to different tribes due to family, geography, interests, and ideology, we all belong to the tribe of humanity.

Unmask Your Ideological Persona

Unmask your ideological persona by listing everything that you believe and value. Examine the labels you use to define yourself and explore the differences between empirically provable facts and your chosen beliefs.

In ancient Greece, Plato extolled the virtues of living an examined life. Too many people parrot their beliefs and values without ever taking a closer look. Their ideological persona has come together almost through happenstance.

Unmasking what you believe and where those beliefs came from can be an eye-opening experience. Even those who think they have chosen their beliefs carefully can benefit from this exercise and make surprising discoveries.

Rethink Your Use of Ideological Labels

Language is labeler-in-chief. Simply pointing to something and identifying it with a word is an act of labeling.

As such, labels (however incomplete) are extremely helpful shortcuts. They allow humans to communicate about everything from nuanced physical science to emotional states and abstract ideas.

Still, as we have explored in this movement, excessive and aggressive ideological labeling can backfire and cause deepening divides. With that in mind, rethink your use. Examine when labeling helps and when it hurts.

For example, in one of my workshops, two doctors started talking about the use of disease labels. They both agreed that labels could be helpful diagnostic tools but that when patients start clinging to those labels (as in "my [disease name]"), it could often backfire and prevent patients from getting better. Analytical labels were never supposed to become an integral part of someone's identity.

Another participant proposed a funky thought experiment that is worth sharing. He asked us to imagine what would happen if we approached everyone we met like they had a Ph.D. in physics (or something else we value). How would we treat them differently, he asked. Try it and see for yourself.

In addition, look to your personal experiences for more samples. Have you, for instance, ever used labels to describe another person and later found out that you were wrong? What did that feel like and how did it change your thinking? What about the opposite, that is, other people labeling you and being wrong? What did that feel like? Document your answers for clarity.

Obviously, there is a time and place to employ labels in our communications, but when we are dealing with ideological differences, it can be helpful to slow down, ask questions, and consider nuance rather than paint everything black and white with simple narratives and easy to apply stickers.

MOVEMENT 2: PARTICIPATE IN CO-HUMAN EXPERIENCES

Overview

- Co-human experiences can reduce anxiety, build trust, increase empathy and change perceptions
- Facilitated events include eating together, doing good works, playing games, creating, worshipping side-by-side, and more
- For best results, set aside ideologies and focus on human commonalities
- The goal is to create safe spaces for human-to-human contact

The premise for shared human experiences is fairly simple. If people can be around each other doing co-human things—i.e., things that everyone does, such as eating food, helping others, creating, talking about their family, sharing their life story, etc. — and not feel threatened, anxieties are reduced, empathy is increased, trust is built, and perceptions are changed.

Dr. Martin Luther King Jr. was resolute in his conviction that people of different creeds and colors need to be around each other, stating with a passion that:

"Men often hate each other because they fear each other; they fear each other because they don't know each other; they don't know each other because they can not communicate; they can not communicate because they are separated."

They are separated.

His was an accurate observation. Birds of a feather flock together. People self-segregate. This is both natural and normal so long as it is not coerced. Individuals choose to be around others who are like them. And yet, most folks make a noteworthy discovery when they set aside visual and ideological distinctions and mingle with people who they previously thought of as completely different, essentially, that they have more in common than they realized.

This has been my experience with all types of interfaith events. Due to my active engagement, I have had an opportunity to spend time with people of all faiths, which here means all strongly held beliefs, since atheists, humanists and those who call themselves spiritual-but-not-religious also attend these events, albeit in smaller numbers.

In hindsight, I can safely say that my involvement has changed my perceptions more than I had expected. Every time I drive home from one of these events, a sense of connectedness lingers, subtle anxieties that I didn't know existed about visual or ideological differences have been reduced, my ability to empathize with those who espouse different beliefs has increased, and I feel hopeful about the human race.

One would think that something amazing would have needed to have taken place to create such fantastic results or that I was somehow special in my ability to relate with others.

Neither is true.

Interactions during these interfaith gatherings are usually rather mundane. In fact, what is unique about them is their *mundaneness*.

Imagine going to an event with a sense of trepidation, thinking that everyone there is going to be completely different from you. Initially, you would only see those differences, including different garbs and religious wear, different races, different accents, and so on. However, as you'd begin to mingle and interact, you'd find more and more similarities. Little by little you'd realize that all the people there are related through universal co-human elements. They eat like you, laugh like you, think about the weather in the same way, talk about their feelings and families, feel the need for safety, and down the list you go. The experience is ordinary but life-changing at the same time.

Interfaith Thanksgiving Celebration

For the past few years, I have lived with my wife, high-school aged son and tween daughter in a small town south of Austin. There is less diversity here than I would like and that is why I go to Austin for interfaith events. Since most of the gatherings are scheduled on school nights, I usually go alone, but in 2017 I decided to bring my family with me to the annual iACT Thanksgiving Celebration. It was held at Riverbend Church and was hosted by the Muslim community.

Before I continue with the story, can I draw your attention to that for a moment? A Christian church opened its doors to the Muslim community to host an event in their house of worship because the Muslims did not have facilities that were large enough to accommodate all those who were interested. In some parts of the world, this kind of behavior would have raised eyebrows or been frowned upon, but in Austin, it was just another day of harmonious relations that underscored years of tireless interfaith work.

The two-hour service was inspiring, filled with prayers for peace and beautiful music from a variety of traditions. Leaders representing Islam, Judaism, a variety of Christian denominations, Hinduism, Sikhism, Bahaism, and Buddhism gave their blessings and spoke about the importance of purposely interacting with one another. Afterward, attendees were treated to a cultural festival that included food and music from a variety of predominantly Muslim countries.

My family loved the entire experience. They were delighted by the messages of hope and harmony, the music, the food, the crowd—all of it. On our way home, we were having a conversation about what we had seen and I asked my son what had stood out to him. He replied: "They weren't anything like what they're portrayed as on TV."

To understand the context in which that statement was uttered, we have friends who are Hindus, Buddhists, Christians, atheists, and agnostics, but he had never met anyone of the Islamic faith before. He had only seen Muslims portrayed on television shows... probably not in a positive light.

Think about that. His fifteen-year-old mind had just been opened up to a less threatening reality than the one he had been exposed to up until that point in his life.

Since then, I've used this example in many of my workshops and capped it off by saying: "That's it! That's all that needs to happen. A slight reduction of anxieties, a new perception, a sense of empathy, a mere act of one human persona seeing another human persona and making a subtle subconscious connection."

From Iceland to Texas

When I moved from Iceland to Texas in 2010, I was forced to face several unconscious and uncharacteristically judgmental attitudes.

In Iceland, I had labeled myself a political moderate and my voting history included both center-right and center-left political parties (plural, as in, there are a lot of political parties in Iceland, not just the two choices we have here in the USA).

Furthermore, I stood outside of organized religion as a part of the spiritual-but-not-religious movement. I thought of myself as fairly evolved spiritually and predominantly free of pejorative views.

Yet, after we arrived, I struggled mightily with many of the religious and political ideologies I was faced with in Texas. For a while there, I couldn't even get myself to interact with people who showed different ideological preferences.

Thank goodness for my wife and kids.

Because of my children, who were two and seven when we moved to Texas, I've interacted with a number of parents through everything from sports and band to Girl Scouts and Mu Sool Won. Furthermore, my wife, who is a natural connector, has brought me along to crawfish boils, dinner clubs, game nights, and more.

Through these interrelations, I have realized that many of my assumptions were wrong. Mingling with an assortment of nice people in Texas—people who have beliefs and values that are different from my own, but who treat everyone around them with dignity and respect—has been eye-opening.

The exposure has allowed me to see nuance where I saw none before and to connect directly with ideological rivals through our shared humanity. I've even made friends with several individuals that I would never have socialized with in Iceland. While they are of a different tenor than ones with which I achieve ideological parity, I enjoy our interactions nonetheless.

In my native Icelandic, the word *heimskur* is synonymous with stupidity but has a slightly different meaning. Directly translated the word means *homeish*, i.e., someone who only knows his or her backyard. Stupidity denotes a lack of intellectual capacity while homeishness indicates a lack of exposure to other cultures, people with different ideologies, a variety of surroundings, and so on. A homeish person is not intellectually challenged but has been confined to home and has a limited view of the world as a result.

While I had traveled to Europe, lived in Australia for a year, and been to several places in America before I moved to Texas, I was homeish (limited) when it came to my views about the people who lived in the Lone Star State. A few of my predispositions turned out to be true, but most of them did not. There were always more nuanced beliefs to be found and more to the story than I had anticipated.

Becoming aware of my underlying biases was one of the reasons why I trained to become an Interfaith Minister, and it was most certainly a contributing factor to the formation of Harmony Interfaith Initiative. In fact, if I had not moved to Texas, I guarantee I would not have written this book.

I am not alone in making such discoveries. I recently read an opinion piece by Ann Bauer in the Washington Post titled, *'I was a Yankee liberal. It took moving to Arkansas for me to understand my biases,'* that detailed many of the same experiences I had. She was, for example, willing to overlook steadfast and sometimes judgmental beliefs held by her friends who were vegan and Muslim, but wasn't willing to do the same for conservative Christians, that is, until she found herself interacting with them on a daily basis. It's astounding what regular interactions can do.

The bottom line is that there are plenty of good people who oppose my ideological beliefs and there are plenty of unpleasant people who share my views. Reality is not one-sided.

Anxiety, Trust, Empathy, and Perceptions

In the introduction to this movement, I used four words to underscore the importance of co-human experiences: *trust, empathy, perceptions,* and *anxiety.* It's time to offer more detailed definitions, starting with the Merriam-Webster dictionary designations:

- **Anxiety**: Apprehensive uneasiness or nervousness, usually over an impending or anticipated ill
- **Trust**: Reliance on the character, ability, strength, or truth of someone or something
- **Empathy**: The action of understanding, being aware of, being sensitive to, and vicariously experiencing the feelings, thoughts, and experiences of another
- **Perception**: A capacity for comprehension, a mental image

When people feel anxiety, it revolves around an anticipated ill. Anticipation requires imagination, which means that feelings of anxiety arise because of an imagined outcome based on the information that we have already gathered through our perception. When the information is wrong or our perception limited, we experience unnecessary anxiety. For example, if you've never met a person of a particular faith or ideological disposition, then all you have to go on is your imagination and that is limited by your experiences, conversations, and quite often colored by the news or images you gather. Since news outlets primarily focus on the disruption of harmony, they serve as an unreliable source that can easily increase anxiety.

This is why anxiety and perceptions go hand in hand. In the same way that we need to taste a variety of fruits and sugary products to pinpoint the concept of sweetness, *we need to interact with a variety of people to perceive our sense of co-humanity.*

Once we are able to modify our perceptions through direct interactions, we reduce levels of anxiety because we no longer anticipate based on incomplete information.

When it comes to trust, most people have developed fairly acute ways to measure honesty in personal interactions. It's not an exact science, and some people are better at it than others, but, in general, human beings have the ability to read body language, tone of voice, use of words, and more, to gauge whether or not a person is being truthful. While measuring truthfulness and trustworthiness is never easy, it is easier to do via personal interactions than from afar. For instance, how many times have you heard someone say: "This man seems nice enough, but I'll have to meet him in person to see whether or not I can trust him." That is how direct co-human experiences can influence trust or lack thereof.

To be able to empathize, we have to attempt to see the world from other people's perspectives. We may never be able to know exactly how another feels, but we can come close by trying to see the world from their point of view. It goes without saying that it's easier to imagine interior sensations after we've had face-to-face encounters. Looking at a picture or reading someone's story can certainly be helpful, and I encourage that type of empathizing, but nothing really substitutes direct human-to-human contact.

With these definitions in mind, we can see how co-human experiences have the potential to change perceptions, reduce anxiety, build trust, and increase capacity for empathy.

What Kind of Experiences?

Once you've recognized the importance of engaging in co-human experiences, you need to decide what type of interactions you want to facilitate or participate in. As previously stated, co-human experiences can revolve around anything that brings people together at the human level, in essence, events where human personas can interact without being forced to either defend or disseminate ideological viewpoints.

I used to think that going to events where the main goal was to mingle and get to know the everyday aspects of other people's lives was a waste of time. My goal was always to get into deep ideological conversations where I could either resonate with people's ideas or prod them to explain or defend their points of view. While I still enjoy interesting ideological discussions, I was wrong to dismiss commonplace human elements. *Exploring co-humanity is never a waste of time.* In fact, it seems to be the only doorway that will open up a possibility for respectful ideological exchanges.

On the following pages, I will provide several examples of co-human encounters. Hopefully, this will get you started. Just remember that getting people together is a creative process and that the only thing that limits your options is your own imagination.

Eating Together

Breaking bread. Sitting down for a meal together. These are probably the oldest forms of human experience. We all need to eat, so why not use that time to connect with other people? Meals have been used to broker peace during times of war, settle personal disputes, reconnect estranged family members, deepen romantic connections, create strong business alliances, fan the embers of love, and much more. Food can be central in our efforts to create co-human experiences. Even when our primary focus is not to gather for a meal, it's always a good idea to feed people when they come together. More than ninety percent of the interreligious, interfaith, and interideological events I have attended have included food as a major component. Whether it's a potluck, a three-course meal, coffee and cookies, or something more elaborate, food always brings people together.

For instance, I am on the advisory board for Dialogue Institute Austin, which was founded by Turkish-American Muslims. Early on, they got into the habit of preparing delicious meals before every dialogue. It was never meant to be the main attraction, but attendees loved their food so much that they went home and told their friends: "Oh, you have to go. The food is wonderful." Instead of fighting against the perception, they decided to embrace the role of food and placed it front and center. Great food now has become synonymous with their dialogue program and all the other events that they offer to get people together.

Doing Good Works Together

Imagine this. You are working at a food drive to help the less fortunate. You look to one side and find someone of a different faith. You look to the other side and find someone of a different ideological persuasion. You realize that none of that matters. You are doing good works side-by-side and understand that helping people is the only reason why all of you have come together.

iACT was founded on the premise of *"people of different faiths doing good together."* In addition to their superb dialogue program, the Austin based organization runs a volunteer program where people of all faiths and persuasions come together to fix houses for those who cannot afford to do so on their own. Participants have told me that the connection created between helpers is sustained well after the good deed is done and some have made friends for life.

In Memphis, MIFA (Metropolitan Inter-Faith Association) regularly hosts youth groups of different faiths. They begin their interactions by engaging in some kind of volunteering—for example, by cleaning up the streets in the surrounding neighborhood—and each volunteer is paired up with someone of a different faith. Afterward, they have lunch together, play games, and finally, learn a little bit about each other's religion. A MIFA employee, who has become a good friend of mine, told me that adding a service component completely changed these events and brought the kids closer together.

At one of my recent workshops, an attendee told us of a communal shoreline cleanup effort that sparked several good friendships between people of different persuasions. Another attendee told us that she was working with political opponents to create a Veterans Day program in her community.

Whatever the project, there is something magical that happens when people focus on helping others. The poet, Rabindranath Tagore, explained the essence of service orientation eloquently when he wrote:

> *"I slept and dreamt that life was joy.*
> *I awoke and saw that life was service.*
> *I acted and behold, service was joy."*

Worshipping and Meditating Together

While interfaith and interreligious events focus on improving relations between people with strong differing beliefs, multifaith spaces have been popping up all over the world, most notably in airports, for a slightly different purpose. The goal of these spaces is to allow people to worship, pray and meditate side-by-side. While each person stays within the realm of his or her own faith tradition, the activity offers an opportunity to observe co-human elements in action, everything from personal peace and quiet to feelings of elation, quiet sobbing, and stone-faced sincerity. Emotions and physical behaviors have the potential to trigger co-human resonance in others who share the space and generate a sense of harmony.

Learning Together

Elementary schools, high schools, and college campuses offer unique opportunities to interact with people of all faiths and persuasions, even more so than workplaces.

On average, intermingling is more active when kids are younger and becomes more difficult as the ideological persona grows stronger and beliefs solidify.

Organizations such as Interfaith Youth Core and Convergence on Campus have done a great job of facilitating relationships between students, but more can be done so that people don't automatically segregate into ideological camps when they enter higher learning environments.

For the average adult, attending seminars, workshops, and other forms of adult education can create interesting connections between people who wouldn't normally socialize but have similar interests.

As a veteran workshop and seminar facilitator, I can tell you that the connections made in a welcoming learning environment are often more important than the material being presented.

Engaging in Small Talk

Ordinary conversations can be used to deepen co-human connections. For that to happen, the exchanges simply need to be empathetic and revolve around features that we all share as human beings, including lifecycle, health, emotions, kids, work, housing situation, commuting, weather, feelings, entertainment, food, travel, pets, hobbies, family history… or something similar.

I know that I am suggesting small talk and that I shouldn't have to mention it, but, in our age of ideological overemphasizing, we need to remind ourselves of the importance of everyday discussions that people used to take for granted.

Exploring Human Interconnectedness

One way to underline interconnectedness is to take manmade items and wonder how many people it took to create them. Objects of focus can be anything, a pen, table, sandwich, computer, book, or something else. The idea is to discuss every part of the construction, from the extraction or cultivation of the building materials to the manufacturing and distribution process.

In my house, we sometimes play this game at the dinner table and it is astounding to realize how many people have come together to make it possible for us to have a meal. From a single man-made object, we can truly realize that we are never alone and that all human beings are bound together, indebted to their natural environment.

Creating Together

Art offers a unique way to connect with the creative aspect of being human. From flash orchestras for peace (which is a real thing) to pottery and painting, artistic experiences plug into an important element.

All kids are creative until the day that some of them are told that they are artists and others are told they are no good. For those who are not artists, the need for creativity is still there. If we give rise to creativeness in a safe environment and invite people from a variety of backgrounds to join us, the outcome can be magical.

Reading About Others

Not everyone has a chance to interact with diverse groups of people. In some cases, the limitations are geographical, other times people don't have the time.

It may not be the same as meeting people in person, but reading memoirs and biographies with an emphasis on co-humanity can create a special kind of bond. The same can be said about blogs that focus on everyday life and are not heavy on ideology. The information that is gathered through those means can be coupled with imagination and used as a tool for empathy.

Exercising Together

In his book, *The Blue Zones*, Dan Buettner presents findings about health and longevity from communities around the world. One of the insights that he offers is that communal exercising, such as walking or running in groups where the physical exercise is supplemented with personal interactions, has more positive impacts on health than merely exercising alone. We can use that information to our benefit and facilitate co-human experiences through walking, running, yoga, tai chi, cross-fit or other means, using them as meeting places and excuses for healthy co-human activities.

Those who are not in a position to start such groups can achieve similar outcomes by joining their local YMCA.

Playing Games

"Man is man's joy" is a proverb from the *Poetic Edda* that I heard repeated over and over again during my childhood in Iceland. Human beings seek each other's company.

Playing games is probably the oldest pastime in our collective history. From physically active sports to card games and strategy, there is great variety in this field of human endeavor.

For the purposes of engaging co-humanity, age-appropriate and mostly good-natured games need to be chosen, since we don't want to feed the competitive spirit too much and create a new type of divide. The overarching intention is to connect one human persona with another. Again, this may sound simplistic to some, but if people with differing worldviews can play games and laugh a little in each other's company that opens the door for other and more meaningful interactions. Trust is built slowly. Sometimes the first step is to see a glimpse of shared humanity.

Other Experiences

The above examples only scratch the surface of what can be done in the name of co-human experiences. Use your creativity to come up with more ideas.

If You Decide to Facilitate

If you decide to facilitate, remember that you are creating an ideology-free-zone. No politics, religion, or other ideologies are allowed — not for the co-human portion anyway. This is difficult to achieve but of utmost importance. In addition to that, here are a few things to keep in mind:

- Decide whom the experience is for. Is it open to all or do you want to invite specific groups so that they can get to know each other on a co-human level?
- Create a safe space for those you've invited and provide easy access. For that purpose, it matters whether the space you have chosen is neutral, diverse, or represents a certain ideological stance (such as a church or a mosque)
- The appropriate length for these types of experiences ranges from one to three hours, and it is important to plan nearly every minute (even the so-called free time) to help people

stay on track

- Be well-prepared and set parameters based on what you are looking to achieve

Primary Objective and Main Goals

The primary objective is to allow for human-to-human contact. As we've explored, such interactions have the potential to break down barriers and build trust. However, even if none of that is achieved, the mere act of being in each other's presence (so long as it is non-threatening) can have an energetic impact. There is nothing spooky about it; we feel the presence of others. Face-to-face meetings can achieve results that can never be achieved through other means.

Our overarching purpose may be to reduce anxiety, increase trust and empathy, and change perceptions, but we will gladly settle for an outcome where two or more people who disagree with each other on ideological matters have spent time in the same space without showing ill will.

* * *

PERSONAL INITIATIVES

Participate in Co-Human Experiences

Participate in as many co-human experiences as you can. Be around people who have different ideological preferences while doing things that underline your shared humanity. Start with your local interfaith group, then expand your horizons and look for opportunities around you. Use every chance you get to connect through shared humanity and see where it leads.

List Your Ideas for Experiential Events

The ideas we have explored thus far only denote a micro-particle of what is possible. Unleash your imagination and list all the ideas that you have for co-human experiences.

If you come up with something new and amazing that works exquisitely to strengthen human bonds, we, at Harmony Interfaith Initiative, would love to learn about it.

MOVEMENT 3: LEARN AND SHARE THROUGH DIALOGUE

Overview

- Reasons to engage in structured dialogue include: connecting to co-humanity, learning and sharing, persuasion, and conflict resolution
- Focusing on learning and sharing has proven to be most effective when it comes to social harmony
- Structured dialogue guidelines are helpful and there are several options to choose from
- Understand what motivates people to show up by exploring the questions of why, who and where
- Make an effort to refrain from judgment if you decide to facilitate

- Persuasion is a gentle art, not a bulldozer
- Dialogue is the best form of nonviolent conflict resolution

There are four primary reasons to engage in structured dialogue: (1) Talk about human sensibilities and relate with people at a co-human level (small talk), (2) learn about similarities and differences, (3) persuade others, and (4) resolve conflicts, which, depending on their severity, can often benefit from the help of a mediator.

In the public arena, we have plenty of clashes about ideological differences. Citizens, politicians, pundits, and religious leaders are trying to convince people left and right.

Sadly, most of those interactions suffer from a similar malady. People are not listening. Instead, they are launching ideological monologues, or worse, trying to land insults that will make them look good in the eyes of their ideological tribe.

While we need to have clear-eyed discussions about matters that influence everyone's lives and find a balance between freedom to do what we want and responsibility towards those who share the planet with us, there is no conversation to be had until we are willing to listen.

The Importance of Dialogue

It can be hard to see the importance of being exposed to ideas that don't rhyme with ours, especially since we live in a society where most people express themselves with their chosen ideology and channel much of their online activity through a lens of beliefs and values. I, for one, was skeptical about the need for exposure to people of different ideologies for a long time. But, in the same way I realized I was wrong to dismiss everyday interactions as unimportant, I realized that I was wrong to focus only on persuading others without first listening to what they have to say. One of my all-time favorite authors, Ralph Waldo Emerson, wisely wrote that:

"Peace cannot be achieved through violence, it can only be attained through understanding."

There is no better way to achieve understanding than through dialogue. Many have seconded his view, including Fr. Hans Kung, the President for the Foundation of Global Ethic, who said:

"There will be no peace among the nations without peace among the religions and no peace among the religions without dialogue."

Dialogue has proven itself to be the least intrusive and most constructive way to engage with another human being. From early in life, most people are taught to use their words, not their fists, which is a fitting guideline for those who seek to cultivate social harmony.

I confess that I still sense an internal resistance to dialogue from time to time. 'Why bother?' I ask myself. 'Why am I focusing on dialogue instead of taking the fight to those who I disagree with?'

Every time that happens, I remind myself that I'd rather live in a world that values co-human connections and ideological exchanges between opponents than a world that shuns understanding and attempts to manipulate the masses with messages of fear and discord. If escalation were the answer, we would already be moving in the right direction.

Laying the Foundation for Dialogue

Well-meaning people often rush into ideological dialogue about differences and grievances prematurely, without doing the necessary prep work. Keep in mind that sincere dialogue can only take place when people have begun to respect each other. For that to happen, they need to see each other as equally human.

There is no way around it.

So, instead of jumping right into dialogue, remember to grease the wheels with co-human experiences, such as the ones proposed in the previous movement. The mere act of eating together beforehand can be enough to allow people to see glimpses of shared humanity.

That said, more time is usually needed when people are trying to bridge gaping ideological, cultural, and theological divides. Trust is a fickle thing and there is no fixed timeline for establishing it that works across the board.

All you can do is lay the foundation as best you can with co-human experiences before you start to dialogue about differences.

Why Use Structured Guidelines?

When I introduce the importance of structured

dialogue guidelines in my workshops, I sometimes get pushback. "Why can't we just talk to each other?" people ask.

My answer is simple.

There is a time and place for unstructured dialogue and if it happens naturally, simply go with the flow, but sitting people down in a circle, by a table, or facing each other—strangers, who have little in common—and asking them to engage in unstructured dialogue about something, anything, is a recipe for disaster.

Structure allows people to create mutual agreements, generate a conciliatory tone, set clear agendas, have time limits, and more. Participants have freedom to talk about what comes to mind without infringing on others. As such, structure is as important to dialogue as plates and silverware are to fine dining.

Focus on Learning and Sharing

Of the four types of dialogue mentioned earlier, dialogue that is focused on learning and sharing has proven to be the most effective bridge-building technique. It's an approach that encourages the creation of no-pressure zones and gives people exposure to a variety of different perspectives without generating a feeling that they have to change their core beliefs or values.

On the following pages, I will present five tested and proven types of interideological dialogue guidelines that all focus on learning and sharing. Subsequently, we will look at persuasion and conflict resolution.

The Red Bench™ Agreement

My exposure to interfaith dialogue has mainly come through my involvement with iACT, whose volunteers have trained me to be a table host at their Red Bench™ interfaith dialogue events. Being a host is different from being a facilitator because a host takes part in the discussion instead of directing the process like a neutral observer.

At our monthly events, we have discussed topics such as love, hope, home, divine presence, justice, and more. The following is our agreement for a great conversation:

- ✓ Open-mindedness: Listen to and respect all points of view
- ✓ Acceptance: Suspend judgment as best you can
- ✓ Curiosity: Seek to understand rather than persuade; we are not here to "fix" one another
- ✓ Discovery: Question old assumptions, look for new insights
- ✓ Sincerity: Speak to yourself, from your heart, about what has personal meaning to you
- ✓ Brevity: Go for honesty and depth but don't go on and on

When everyone accepts these boundaries, the conversation goes well. I have yet to attend a Red Bench™ dialogue that veered off track. That is thanks to our pledge (above), scripted guidelines, the training that the table hosts receive, and sincere attendees.

Respectful Conversations

The Minnesota Council of Churches created similar guidelines for their *Respectful Conversations* initiative. They urged each participant to:

1. Speak for yourself
2. Practice respect
3. Be brief
4. Listen carefully
5. Respect confidentiality
6. Allow people to pass

If you are interested in seeing a demonstration, the Theater of Public Policy created a short video to illustrate these guidelines. You can find it on YouTube.

Experifaith Dialogue

In my 2017 book, titled *Experifaith: At the Heart of Every Religion*, I explored experiential similarities between religions and urge people to participate in dialogues about their spiritual practices, such as prayer, meditation, worship, service, and more. Here are the dialogue guidelines as they appear in my book:

The Experifaith Agreement

✓ We are willing to share and listen, not

preach or be preached to
- ✓ We are willing to converse on an experiential level
- ✓ We are committed to being cordial in our interactions
- ✓ We will work in harmony towards a better understanding

Before the dialogue begins, I usually read the following passage from Gandhi, but you should feel free to choose a passage that has a similar meaning to you or create your own invocation:

"I offer you peace. I offer you love. I offer you friendship. I see your beauty. I hear your need. I feel your feelings. My wisdom flows from the Highest Source. I salute that source within you. Let us work together for unity and love."

The Experifaith Dialogue Process

- Please limit discussions to how spiritual experiences have influenced your feelings, thoughts and/or actions
- Please refrain from talking about the contents of your belief system, i.e., history, dogma, or orthodoxy. Focus on personal practices and resulting experiences
- Explore both similarities and differences
- Another person's experience cannot be wrong, just different. Even if you find nothing in common with another person, the mere act of trying to understand will reap benefits
- Signal each other by raising your hand if

discussions start to revolve around theology rather than experiences

These types of experiential conversations create a sense of co-humanity. For example, when two people of different faiths talk about the power of prayer in their lives and how the practice has influenced them experientially, they are bound to find similarities. This approach is not meant to belittle obvious differences between religious traditions, such as the content of prayers or whom they are directed at, but rather highlight the fact that while stories and customs vary, human experiences are much the same around the globe.

Ten Interreligious Dialogue Guidelines

Dr. Leonard Swidler is a highly respected scholar in the field of interfaith studies. Based on my research, I can safely say that no one has done more to create parameters for interideological dialogue than he has.

His ten interreligious guidelines go well beyond the scope of religion and can be applied in a wide context to conversations about all types of differences. The following is the short version as Dr. Swidler wrote it. If you want to read his extended version, I urge you to visit the Scarboro Missions website.

1. The primary purpose of dialogue is to learn; that is, to change and grow in the perception and understanding of reality, and then to act accordingly

2. Inter-religious, inter-ideological dialogue must be a two-sided project within each religious or ideological community and between religious or ideological communities

3. Each participant must come to the dialogue with complete honesty and sincerity

4. In inter-religious, inter-ideological dialogue we must not compare our ideals with our partner's practice, but rather our ideals with our partner's ideals, our practice with our partner's practice

5. Each participant must define himself… Conversely, the interpreted must be able to recognize herself in the interpretation

6. Each participant must come to the dialogue with no hard-and-fast assumptions as to where the points of disagreement are

7. Dialogue can take place only between equals… Both must come to learn from each other

8. Dialogue can take place only on the basis of mutual trust

9. Persons entering into inter-religious, inter-ideological dialogue must be at least minimally self-critical of both themselves and their own religious or ideological traditions

10. Each participant eventually must attempt to experience the partner's religion or ideology 'from within'; for a religion or ideology is not merely something of the head, but also of the spirit, heart, and 'whole being,' individual and communal

Because Dr. Swidler's guidelines are so specific, I want to highlight some of the unique aspects that he proposes.

To begin with, his call for comparing ideologies to ideologies, ideals to ideals, and practices to practices is admirable. Using the words that we've been employing in this book so far, he is asking us to compare the ideological persona to the ideological persona and the human persona to the human persona.

His emphasis on self-knowledge is also praiseworthy and rhymes well with what I wrote previously about unmasking the ideological persona. We must know our thoughts, feelings, experiences, and ideals to be able to communicate with another person. Furthermore, when the participant across from us mirrors back what we have said, we must be able to recognize ourselves in the interpretation. If we don't, we need to refine our communications.

The hiccup for most people has to do with presumptions. If we assume we know what the differences and disagreements are going to be about, we come to the dialogue armed with arguments to counter our assumptions and may miss a chance to see the real disagreements.

Finally, being minimally self-critical is a guideline that I have not seen anywhere else, and yet it may be the most important aspect of conducting a dialogue with another human being. People are critical of themselves all the time, often in a demeaning way, but it takes an act of courage and confidence to be slightly critical of one's own beliefs, spiritual principles, humanistic values or religion.

What Dr. Swidler is calling for is the practice of humility. All systems of thinking, even divinely inspired ones, came to be through a human filter and human beings are not perfect. In one of his online videos, he underlines this notion by saying that:

"No one knows everything about anything."

What does he mean by that? Well, to give an example, if there isn't a single person in the world that knows everything about a scientific topic, such as chemistry, then how can anyone claim omniscience about life, the universe, and everything? Taking a minimally self-critical stance does not mean that our entire belief system is wrong. It merely opens a door to the idea that the truth is a vast concept, and that while our piece of the puzzle is important, it is not the entire puzzle.

Here is my abbreviation of Dr. Swidler's ten guidelines, for memorizing:

1. Dialogue to learn
2. Dialogue is between willing participants
3. Be honest and sincere
4. Compare apples to apples
5. Attain self-knowledge; see it mirrored back
6. Make no assumptions about disagreements
7. Dialogue is between equals
8. Dialogue is based on mutual trust
9. Be minimally self-critical
10. Attempt to see the other from within

Counterintuitive Secrets

To throw you a curveball, let me share a list of counterintuitive secrets from the book *Circles of Men* by Clay Boykin, which explains how to run successful spiritual men's groups.

In his research, Clay found that many groups failed because they were too rigid, the men were unwilling to add commitments to an already full calendar, their language was overly structured, and nobody wanted to be fixed. His goal was to create heart-centered connections where men felt safe. In that, he succeeded. Here are some of his secrets along with short explanations:

- Language Matters: Words are at the center of these guidelines
- Framework but Very Little Structure: A rough framework allows participants to decouple from their organized daily lives
- Network instead of Group: Networks are open and fluid while groups tend to be closed
- Intention instead of Commitment: Intention signifies energized focus rather than an unyielding pledge
- Gathering instead of Meeting: Nothing needs to get done or be decided upon when participants are gathering
- Facilitating instead of Leading: The facilitator is not the leader
- Heart over Head: Participants are given permission to release control and move into their hearts

- Conversation instead of Discussion: Having a discussion connotes a conclusion, participants are instead having an open-ended conversation
- Holding Space instead of Fixing: Participants listen to affirm one another with compassion without offering similar stories or trying to fix one another

These secrets are intentionally vague to allow for interpretation, but they convey an overarching sensibility that can be applied to a variety of dialogue situations.

Your Choices Reflect Your Goals

All of these tested and proven guidelines share several similarities. They call for mutual respect, the development of trust, time limits and brevity in interactions, creating room for genuine connections, encouraging authentic communications from a personal or experiential standpoint, and honoring the fact that human beings have two ears and one mouth. The differences between them are also numerous and largely depend on the reason for gathering. Some are flexible while others are rigid, some ask a lot of participants while others ask a little, some are focused on co-human likenesses while others explore ideological distinctions, and so on.

When you choose your approach, make sure that it is in line with the goals that you have set for your gathering. In preparation, ask these essential questions:

- Do we want participants to stay on the surface and focus on cordial co-human interactions or to go deep and explore shared experiences?
- Is our primary goal to create trust between people or explore theological and ideological differences (maybe both)?
- Do we want the conversation to be light and inspiring or do we want to address wounds that need healing?

Your answers will help you to set the tone for your gathering and assist you in deciding which dialogue guidelines to follow.

The Ratio Between Listening and Talking

In their talks, the three Interfaith Amigos—Imam Jamal Rahman, Pastor Don Mackenzie, and Rabbi Ted Falcon—provide a comical reenactment of their first encounters by talking over each other. "My scripture this, my tradition that…" was pretty much all they could say to each other in the beginning. However, their relationship began to improve significantly when they started listening deeply. Now they travel the world and convey lessons that they have learned from their interactions, the most important of which is to listen. In our search for harmony, listening and learning about the other comes first while sharing comes second. Listening is crucial.

I'll admit that this focus on listening has been extremely difficult for me. I still haven't mastered the two ears to one mouth ratio, probably because

I have been a public speaker for most of my adult life and I usually have something to say. I am aware of this shortcoming and practice listening every chance I get. Asking questions is the most potent tool at my disposal. It has also been tremendously helpful to be vulnerable about my tendency and catch myself publicly when I stray off track by saying something like, "Oops! There I go again," which has the added benefit of being a confusing reference to two popular songs.

I share this personal admission to underscore the importance of self-awareness and practice. Even with the best of intentions, all of us can fall into familiar patterns during conversations. Our attempt to apply unfamiliar dialogue principles takes practice and sincere willingness.

Whenever I am tempted to appear perfect in my interactions with others, I remind myself of this passage by David D. Burns, MD, one of the pioneers of cognitive behavioral therapy:

"Aim for success, not perfection. Never give up your right to be wrong, because then you will lose the ability to learn new things and move forward with your life. Remember that fear always lurks behind perfectionism. Confronting your fears and allowing yourself the right to be human can, paradoxically, make yourself a happier and more productive person."

What Motivates People to Show Up?

Once you have chosen a topic, set goals for your interactions, and decided on the dialogue guidelines that best suit the situation, you need to find a way to bring people together. That's not easy. As stated earlier, birds of a feather flock together. People like their comfort zones. You are competing with busy schedules and easy access to entertainment. In that atmosphere, you need to address motivations with a special focus on answering *why*, *who* and *where* questions.

Let's start with *why*. Why should people spend their valuable time improving relations through dialogue? Anthony Robbins is an expert on this topic and says that motivation usually boils down to a combination of pleasure and pain, be it physical, emotional, or mental. If people feel badly enough, they will want to do something to reduce the hurt, and if they have started seeing positive outcomes, they will want more of those. The key is to speak to other people's pain and pleasure when you reach out, not to your own.

That brings us to the questions of *who* and *where*. It has been my experience that attendance is often related to location and leadership. For example, people who attend places of worship that are hosting particular events usually show up in larger numbers than those who come from the outside. It also matters who is in attendance. When church leaders show up, many from their flock come with them. When mayors and police chiefs attend, constituents often show up as well. Targeting certain groups and leaders while also making sure that the location is suitable are two key ingredients for attracting people to interideological and interfaith events.

The most important thing is to continually look for ways to broaden the appeal of dialogue rather than alienate people we disagree with or have a hard time reaching. The goal must be to increase diversity. Not everyone will attend these types of events but, if the work continues, they will eventually know someone who has and that can make all the difference. Remember, we only need one or two dedicated bridge-builders per group of 40-120.

Develop Personal Relationships

There is no substitute for creating personal relationships when it comes to expanding reach and increasing diversity. I urge you to make an effort to get to know at least one person at every event you attend and then slowly build your relationship through continued interactions. Call it co-human networking.

I've met several people over coffee after interfaith events and have usually walked away with a stronger sense of our human connection. To give you a unique example, I met a Muslim activist at an interfaith gathering early in 2018 who wasted no time when I sent him a follow-up email and invited my entire family for brunch with his family. It was a joyous experience and we have become good friends since. If you reach out, you never know what will happen.

Sincere Dialogue Facilitation

The guidelines for facilitating dialogue are similar to the guidelines for facilitating co-human experiences. Set an intention, be well prepared, outline the agreement (dialogue guidelines), stay on track, and respect time limits. What sets dialogue apart from co-human experiences is that people may express ideas and relay incidents that are difficult to listen to for one reason or another. Most of the time you can simply move on to the next person, but there are times when you have to take action, either by addressing what has been said or stop the person in question from sharing for the good of the group.

While this is exceedingly rare, especially when people have come to the dialogue willingly and agreed to the dialogue guidelines beforehand, you have to be prepared. The most important thing is to stay calm and refuse to intensify the situation.

Overall, participants can be passionate, introverted, curious, seemingly uninterested, and everything in between. *Don't dismiss anyone.* Your role is not to make judgments about participants but allow them to share and keep the conversation going. Direct contact with many personality types is just as important as exposure to many points of view. Give people space to make up their own mind about what they have seen and heard.

During my twenty years as a yoga instructor, my primary purpose for each class was to create a safe space for my students. Many elements go into the creation of a safe space, including the teacher's demeanor, his or her control of the class (if students feel like someone else is in control, they don't feel safe), temperature, settings, cleanliness, access, professionalism or lack thereof, and more.

Ever since I entered the interfaith arena, I have approached dialogue facilitation from the same angle, focusing on the creation of safe spaces where people feel that they can open up and share with each other.

All that being said, let me reiterate one thing. Facilitators don't have to be perfect. If you are facilitating dialogue and you mess up, you mess up. Say you're sorry and move on. Instead of aiming for perfection, strive for sincerity.

What If You Want to Persuade?

What if you disagree vehemently with another person? What can you do to make them see things your way? The short answer to that question is: Nothing. You can't make anyone do anything, least of all change his or her mind.

However, if you earnestly want to persuade someone, here are several insights from Megan Phelps-Roper who gave an inspiring TED talk about her shift away from extremism. She was raised in the Westboro Baptist Church, which, for those who don't know, is a controversial church that exults in demonizing those who don't follow the word of God (her description). Her earliest memory of the church's activism was when she was five years old, standing on a street corner in Kansas holding a sign that read: "Gays are worthy of death."

I will not recount her entire story in this book—her TED talk is riveting and well worth your time—but it suffices to say that through persistent online interactions with people who disagreed with her, she changed her mind, left the church, and now works as a writer and educator on topics related to extremism, bullying, and empathy. To better understand why and how she changed her mind, she unveiled four things that the people who persuaded her did differently and now presents them as guidelines for others. The following is my slightly rephrased version:

- **Don't assume bad intent:** Even when people are professing to ideologies that you vigorously disagree with, assume that they are trying to do the right thing in the best way they know how. Supposing bad intent makes us forget our shared humanity and cuts off the possibility for understanding.

- **Ask questions:** Effective counterarguments cannot be made unless there is an understanding of where the other side is coming from. Asking questions helps us map the disconnect and signals to the other person that he or she is being heard.

- **Stay calm:** As you can imagine, staying calm takes practice and patience while dialing up the rhetoric will inflame the conversation and can end with a bang. Tell a joke, excuse yourself from the conversation, or take a deep breath, but refuse to escalate.

- **Make the argument:** People who have strong beliefs often assume that the value of their position is obvious and self-evident. We need to be willing to make the argument for our point of view instead of presenting our preferred ideology as fact.

When it works—and let me restate that it infrequently does—persuasion is a gentle and patient art rather than a bulldozer. Too many people are engaged in head-on collisions these days. Using this tempered approach to persuasion is a step in the right direction.

Just remember that the ideological persona can make argument after argument without making a dent in another person's thinking unless the human persona has been engaged in a meaningful way. Remarkably enough, Megan Phelps-Roper's humanity was engaged in the digital space, showing that it is possible to be co-human there, even though it is harder to do than in face-to-face meetings.

With all of that being said, I have long lived by the words of author and motivational speaker Dale Carnegie, who said that:

"A man convinced against his will, is of the same opinion still."

I usually back off when I meet strong ideological resistance in someone I don't know. The reason? I have not had a chance to engage his or her human persona successfully. Based on my experience, no one will get convinced of anything except his or her own righteousness if an argument keeps intensifying. Incessantly pressing my point could endanger an opportunity to engage with the human persona in my ideological opponent—maybe forever.

As much as people would like to believe that everyone can be persuaded like Megan Phelps-Roper was, persuasion usually doesn't come from the outside. Whether you are a Zen trainee, corporate board member, religious zealot, or political activist, change usually comes from the inside. For illustration, it's good to remember that an eggshell broken from the outside signals destruction while an eggshell broken from the inside denotes the beginning of a new life.

Resolving Differences

People have disagreements. That's just the way life is. Individuals fight, families fight, neighbors fight, countries fight… and on it goes.

Hanna Arendt, who was a renowned German philosopher, said that the behavior that makes human beings unique is our capacity for forgiveness. The desire for vengeance is automatic and animalistic, but forgiveness requires real thought-out action that releases both the forgiver and the forgiven. Forgiveness is miracle-like in its ability to transform worldly situations and nullify past actions. Having the ability to forgive is a true blessing.

Even so, certain differences are more difficult to forgive, resolve, or move past than others. In those cases, the justice system sometimes needs to get involved. Some incidents go to court, whereas others are resolved with the assistance of a mediator.

When I was researching for this book, I visited a professor at a nearby college that teaches mediation. I was hoping to get access to tricks-of-the-trade that I could share with my readers. What I found was a nuanced field that relies heavily on skill and training. There are no universal tips that can be applied to every situation. That being said, I did garner two insights from the professor that I thought worth sharing.

First, when seeking solutions, try to put aside personalities and history. Focus instead on facts and competing interests. It is much easier to talk about the issues than argue for or against subjective likability or be preoccupied with a past that cannot be changed. Temperaments and preceding events tend to ignite passions rather than reason.

Second, dive deeper into competing interests by asking the question: What do they actually want?

The professor offered me an example. He asked me to imagine that I have two kids (which I do) and that both of them want the last orange in the house. The quick and easy way to resolve that situation would be to cut the orange in half and be done with it. But, he said, a mediator takes time to *dig deeper*. If, for example, the parent finds out that one kid needs the orange peel for a cake recipe and the other needs the orange seeds for a growing experiment, then cutting the orange in half would serve neither. In fact, by looking deeper, the parent can give both kids precisely what they are looking for.

These two insights represent a fraction of what mediation is all about.

If you need to seek help, you will get assistance from trained professionals who seek non-combative resolutions to difficult disputes.

Thankfully, mediation is the fastest growing profession in the legal system.

Make a Commitment to Dialogue

Whether you intend to connect via discussions about similar experiences, learn and share, gently persuade, or resolve differences, I urge you to make a commitment to dialogue.

The opposite approach is just too dangerous. It can be easy to forget the lessons of history, including the tragedies of war, and ramp up divisive and destructive rhetoric without concern for the consequences.

Those of us who are committed to harmony and bridge-building need to offer alternative methods. Dialogue still reigns supreme as a method for connection and conflict resolution.

* * *

PERSONAL INITIATIVES

Drill Down on Why

Before you bring other people into the mix, drill down on your *why*. Why do you want to engage in dialogue? Many goal-setting exercises encourage people to ask "Why?" five times to get to the source of their motivation. "Why do you want this?" "Because of that?" "Why do you want that?" "Because of…" and so on, five times.

Once you've discovered your unique set of reasons, you'll have access to a wellspring of enthusiasm that will keep you going through adversity.

Use Dialogue Guidelines With Friends

Try using some of the previously mentioned dialogue guidelines in conversations with your friends and acquaintances (for example, within a church community or spiritual group) before you attempt to use them in larger settings. Choose appropriate guidelines, make an agreement, discuss a topic, and then review the process to see what went well and what you struggled with. Ask every question you can think of to examine the process and evaluate it for yourself. Once you feel comfortable, you can use the same guidelines with strangers in more diverse situations.

Attend Dialogue Sessions (if available)

Densely populated areas in the USA usually offer some sort of interfaith or interreligious dialogue programs and you should be able to find what you are looking for with a simple Internet search. For those who live away from urban areas, smaller interideological programs are being run across the country, and you may find one in your area. It can be quite daunting to enter this realm for the first time. Attend with an open mind and see what you find.

Don't Take Words Too Personally

Interideological dialogue is hard enough without people being too sensitive. It goes without saying that most aggressive forms of name-calling and labeling should be confronted, but refrain from misinterpreting people's words and gestures as insults. Offer gentle feedback instead of responding with indignation. Most of all, give people the benefit of the doubt.

Create Your Own Guidelines

Make a list of all the elements that you deem important from the five guidelines offered in this book and use them as inspiration to create your own dialogue guidelines. This exercise can inform your approach to interactions in the future and give you a sense of what is important to you in structured settings, even if you never use your method to orchestrate a dialogue of your own.

List Important Topics

"Why aren't people talking about [fill in the blank]?" If you can't find groups who are talking about the topics that you are really interested in, then do yourself a favor and list all the topics that you want to discuss. Once you have the list, you can either suggest them as topics at your local interfaith gathering or moderate dialogues of your own.

To Host or Not to Host?

That brings us to the final initiative. Should you host a dialogue session or not? That depends. Do you have a burning desire? Do you have access to space? Are there enough people in your circle of influence to generate interest?

I've heard of successful dialogue programs that were launched through Meetup.com and some that started in living rooms. Inversely, I've heard of unsuccessful programs that were initiated by large organizations that had not done the necessary footwork to prepare.

Success is not determined by size. If you choose to go for it, remember these three words: Preparation, Persistence, and Patience.

MOVEMENT 4: NURTURE HARMONY FROM WITHIN

Overview

- Harmony begins within
- Self-care can lead to world-care
- Each person can choose his or her path but must remain aware of unconscious pitfalls, such as the attraction-repulsion principle
- The five moderating behaviors are (1) emphasis on attraction, (2) awareness, (3) humility, (4) humor, and (5) slowing down to understand

As the previous movements have shown, there are many things we can do to support and further the cause of social harmony. However, without the fourth movement, our efforts may fall short. Before we can harmonize with others, we must first tune our own instrument.

"If we could change ourselves, the tendencies in the world would also change. As a man changes his own nature, so does the attitude of the world change towards him. We need not wait to see what others do."

This Mohandas K. Gandhi quote was later shortened, supposedly by his grandson, Arun Gandhi, into the better known:

"Be the change you want to see in the world."

The latter version is usually attributed to the elder statesman, but the younger Gandhi, who is still alive and working on his grandfather's mission today, is said to have simplified the proclamation to solidify his grandfather's main teachings.

Both versions point to a great truth.

Harmony begins within. If we are to influence the world around us, even in minor ways, the real work begins inside and emanates outwards. We don't need to be perfect to do good deeds in the world, but we need to be sincere in our efforts. If we are in continual states of discord (i.e., outraged, negative, demanding, judgmental, spiteful, etc.) and try to promote harmony at the same time, emotional turbulence will sabotage our integrity and people will not listen.

To paraphrase Emerson, 'how people act speaks so loudly that we can't hear what they are saying.'

For best results, harmony should resonate from within, and an alignment of thought, word and deed is preferable.

From Self-Care to World-Care

Carol Gilligan's model for moral development shows that human beings generally move from being selfish to being able to care for others in their near environment to, in rare cases, showing genuine care for people they don't know.

When we compare her model to others in the same vein—including Piaget, Loevinger, Erikson, Steiner, Beck, Graves, Kohlberg, Peck, Fowler, Wilber and others—moral growth corresponds with people's ability to see the world from an ever-increasing number of perspectives and act accordingly; a classification that rhymes with the human ability for compassion, defined as *the sympathetic consciousness of others' distress together with a desire to alleviate it.*

Simply put, moral growth leads to increased compassion and care, both of which are central to the development of social harmony.

Let's take a quick look at the progression.

At stage one, a person that is selfish can only see the world from his or her point of view. The healthy version of selfishness produces self-care and win-win situations while the unhealthy version produces battles and win-lose scenarios, where selfish desires are achieved at other people's expense. Society has a number of names for this behavior, including narcissism, vanity, egotism, and self-absorption. While selfishness is generally frowned upon, it is often celebrated in popular culture.

At the second stage, individuals are generous towards those who are within their circle of care, including spouses, family, and friends. A person that has begun to care for another is willing to sacrifice time, energy, and money unselfishly so that another may grow and flourish (M. Scott Peck's definition of love). The ability to care for others epitomizes the underpinnings of civilized society. Without a tapestry of caring, civilization would collapse into a chaotic every-man-for-himself battlefield.

The third stage of development, world-care, is relatively uncommon. It depends on people's ability to show care and compassion for others they do not know. World-care can start with minor things, such as a genuine willingness to pay taxes for the greater good or reducing personal consumption to curb carbon emissions, but, as empathy grows, people at the stage of world-care will genuinely attempt to care for everyone, often at their own expense.

Later in this movement, we will take a look at four examples of this behavior, including Gandhi, Mother Teresa, Nelson Mandela, and Betty Williams, three of whom won the Nobel Peace Prize and one who deserved to but was never awarded.

For world-care to be authentic, it has to spring from an internal stage of moral development, not from an external dictate. Many high-minded ideals have failed in the public square because moral development was not factored into the equation—especially the hold that selfishness has over most people—nor was there made an intentional effort to foster people's capabilities for empathy, care, and growth.

Expanding the Circle of Care

If individuals want to increase their aptitude for care and compassion, they need to establish self-care and then expand their abilities outwards. The most common metaphors for the first step are:

a) Learn how to swim before you attempt to rescue a drowning person

b) When pressure falls in an airplane cabin, put the oxygen mask on yourself first and then on your child

c) You have to earn money before you can give money

d) Demonstrate love for those who are near you before you attempt to love the entire world

The underlying principle is always the same. Caring is an ability. If you cannot care for yourself, how can you care for others? Expanding the circle of care looks something like this:

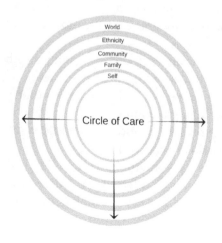

Each successive circle denotes an increased ability to care for more and more people.

Simultaneously, each expansion asks for additional sacrifices; a term used here in the dictionary definition, to connote a *willingness to give up something valued for the sake of something else regarded as more important or worthy.*

The aspect of sacrifice is essential in the context of care. You cannot, for example, say that you care for your young children and then desert them to focus on fulfilling your selfish needs. Every parent knows that sleepless nights and inevitable changes in the social calendar come with having children. Levels of difficulty may differ depending on the needs of the child, but there is always some sacrifice involved.

Likewise, people who have devoted their lives to establishing social harmony and peaceful coexistence have often made tremendous sacrifices.

With this in mind, ask yourself: "How far am I willing to go in the expansion of my circle of care?" There is no right or wrong answer here. Nobody is holding a gun to your head telling you to grow morally and care for others at your own expense.

For instance, there is nothing inherently wrong with deciding that you want to focus primarily on self-care. By taking care of yourself (without taking advantage of others) you won't be a burden on society and may end up contributing to the world around you.

Nor is there anything wrong with focusing all your energy on your family. World peace could be easily achieved if everyone took good care of their children and loved their relatives.

The question of how much you are willing to sacrifice only has significance when your aptitude for empathy is sufficiently developed and you feel a personal need to expand your circle of care and compassion. Once you *decide* to grow and expand, however, step into the role with open eyes like a willing parent who is ready to accept both the challenges and joys that come with caring for others. Be hopeful for our potential as human beings and forgiving of our inherent flaws.

India's Great Soul

Mohandas K. Gandhi (1869-1948) was a towering figure in history. He lived his philosophy of nonviolent resistance (satyagraha) to the best of his ability. His approach, which grew into a full-fledged ideology with many specific tenets, was primarily based on acts of self-control, developing peace from within, and standing firm when it came to righteous convictions, never at the expense of others but always at one's own expense. He preached that satyagrahis should never hate the doer, only resist the action, and that no human being was beyond redemption, repeatedly stating that:

"It is easy enough to be friendly to one's friends. But to befriend the one who regards himself as your enemy is the quintessence of true religion. The other is mere business."

As a lawyer, activist, spiritual figure, and politician, Gandhi was not beyond reproach, but looking at his life, one can hardly doubt the sincerity of his convictions nor argue against their effectiveness.

His road from self-care to world-care began with a spiritual upbringing in India and a legal education in England. Pride was the seed that flowered into a lifetime of activism. After buying a first-class train ticket via mail, Gandhi was thrown out of his prepaid cabin and off the train for being Indian. That so insulted his dignity that he went to work for the civil rights of the Indian community in South Africa. It was there, with inspiration from Thoreau, among others, that he developed his philosophy of nonviolent civil disobedience.

During that time he also emphasized good relations between religions, which became an ongoing theme throughout his life:

"If we are to respect others' religions, as we would have them respect our own, a friendly study of the world's religions is a sacred duty."

After success in South Africa, Gandhi returned to India and expanded his circle of care to include the Indian people who quickly bestowed on him the honorary title Mahatma, which means great (Maha) soul (Atman). He spent most of his adult life working towards Indian independence at a tremendous personal expense. Sacrifice was really at the heart of his philosophy; the will to suffer until the suffering became unbearable in the eyes of the oppressors.

Partly thanks to his efforts, India finally gained independence in 1947, one year prior to his assassination.

In the final year of his life, Gandhi kept wanting to expand his circle of care to include all of the world's inhabitants and was increasingly worried about world peace, but, since his life was cut short, we will never know what kind of work he would have engaged in for the purpose of co-human harmony.

Today, Gandhi is a revered historical figure, sometimes to the point of deification (especially in India), but he was simultaneously an exceptional servant of humanity and a flawed human being. He readily admitted to some of those flaws in his autobiography while other shortcomings have been exposed in the light of modern values.

What we can surmise from Gandhi's story is this. Without a modicum of self-care—including a spiritual upbringing and high-quality education—he would not have been prepared to fill his role of service and would likely have failed. Personal pride may have been the instigator for his activism, but he grew into the role and became more selfless with every passing year. His vocation required tremendous sacrifices, especially in regards to his family, as Gandhi spent much of his adult life in and out of prison. His expansion was realized step-by-step by living an intentional life focused on service.

From Housewife to Nobel Laureate

Betty Williams (1943)—who I've quoted several times in this book already—was a fierce proponent of peace in Northern Ireland during the Troubles and won the Nobel Peace Prize in 1976 for co-founding Community of Peace People with Mairead Corrigan and Ciaran McKeown.

There was no shortage of violence in Northern Ireland during the conflict, but the breaking point for Williams and her co-founders was when three children, Joanne (eight-years-old), John (two-and-a-half-years-old), and Andrew (six-weeks-old), were killed during a high-speed chase in West Belfast. *Imagine that.* A young mother was walking her kids down the street on a bright sunny afternoon, her youngest in a stroller, her toddler walking by her side, and her daughter riding a bicycle. Soldiers shot a fleeing man dead and his car plowed into the children outside of St. John the Baptist School. Although Ann Maguire, the mother of the children, survived, the incident so haunted her that she took her own life three and a half years later.

Betty Williams, who was a housewife at the time, resonated deeply with this event. She thought of her own children and how tensions were escalating out of control. Emotions welled up inside of her ("This has to stop!") and caused her to take action. Along with her two co-founders, she started walking the streets, knocking on doors, and asking people to sign a petition that called for an end to violence. The declaration for their organization read:

"We have a simple message to the world from this movement for Peace. We want to live and love and build a just and peaceful society. We want for our children, as we want for ourselves, our lives at home, at work, and at play to be lives of joy and Peace. We recognize that to build such a society demands dedication, hard work, and

courage. We recognize that there are many problems in our society which are a source of conflict and violence. We recognize that every bullet fired and every exploding bomb make that work more difficult. We reject the use of the bomb and the bullet and all the techniques of violence. We dedicate ourselves to working with our neighbors, near and far, day in and day out, to build that peaceful society in which the tragedies we have known are a bad memory and a continuing warning."

People took note. Women flocked to their side. The communal longing for a peaceful resolution was evident. Betty Williams was elevated from housewife to Nobel Peace Prize laureate in a relatively short amount of time. She attributes the success of her initiative to passionate action, which included funneling energy and outrage into walking door to door, marching, and organizing, but she humbly admits that it was also due to the media attention they got because of a slow news season that summer.

Ever since her work began in Northern Ireland, Williams has been actively expanding her circle of care. She heads the Global Children's Foundation and co-founded the Nobel Women's Initiative in 2006. She lectures widely on topics of peace, education, intercultural and interfaith understanding, anti-extremism, and children's rights.

Nun, Teacher, Mother, Saint

Mother Teresa (1910-1997), born Anjezë Gonxhe Bojaxhiu in Albania, is another Nobel Peace Prize laureate (1979) that is worth mentioning in this context. She left her home in Albania in 1928 to join the Sisters of Loreto in Ireland and become a missionary. That led her to India in 1929 where she taught at St. Teresa's School until she experienced *"the call within the call"* in 1946, at which time she had been helping the poor while living among them during a retreat.

The work for which she is known around the world today began in 1948 and was formally granted permission from the Vatican in 1950 when she founded the Missionaries of Charity. She, along with the sisters in her order, took vows of chastity, poverty, obedience, and wholehearted free service to the poorest of the poor. The first several years of her work were enormously difficult. She had to beg for food and supplies while experiencing loneliness and a yearning for the comforts of convent life. She wrote in her diary:

"The poverty of the poor must be so hard for them. While looking for a home I walked and walked till my arms and legs ached. I thought how much they must ache in body and soul, looking for a home, food and health. Then, the comfort of Loreto [her former congregation] came to tempt me. "You have only to say the word and all that will be yours again," the Tempter kept on saying ... Of free choice, my God, and out of love for you, I desire to remain and do whatever be your Holy will in my regard. I did not let a single tear come."

Thanks to her steadfast devotion, the work continued. She founded hospices where people received medical attention and were given an opportunity to die with dignity in accordance with their faith. Muslims were read the Quran, Hindus received water from the Ganges, and Catholics received final anointing, all in accordance with Teresa's belief that no matter their status in life, people deserved to die like angels—loved and wanted.

By the 1960s, she had opened orphanages, hospices and leper houses throughout India. In 1965, she expanded her congregation abroad and opened a house in Venezuela with five sisters. Her reach increased with every passing year and in 2012, her order had over 4500 sisters active in 133 countries and was managing homes for people dying of HIV/AIDS, leprosy, and tuberculosis, and operating soup kitchens, dispensaries, mobile clinics, family counseling programs, orphanages, and schools. As her circle of care grew Teresa proclaimed:

"By blood, I am Albanian. By citizenship, an Indian. By faith, I am a Catholic nun. As to my calling, I belong to the world."

Mother Teresa was a controversial figure that drew both praise for her work and an array of criticism—much of which was aimed at her rigid belief structure. She was canonized in 2016. Today she is known within the Catholic Church as Saint Teresa of Calcutta.

The Prisoner Who Kept an Open Heart

Nelson Mandela (1918-2013) was a complicated

man. He trained as a lawyer and became an early opponent of apartheid (a system of segregation in South Africa that privileged whites). In his early years, Mandela was attracted to Marxism and wanted to engage in nonviolent protests, but he crossed the line into sabotage against the government in 1961 out of frustration. That was one of the factors used against him when he was sentenced to life in prison for conspiring to overthrow the government. Nevertheless, his commitment to democracy was evident, even at his trial, where he said:

"I have fought against white domination, and I have fought against black domination. I have cherished the ideal of a democratic and free society in which all persons will live together in harmony and with equal opportunities. It is an ideal which I hope to live for and to see realized. But if it need be, it is an ideal for which I am prepared to die."

Mandela spent the next twenty-seven years in prison. He wrote his autobiography in secret during that time and garnered support from people all around the world. Outside pressure mounted until he was finally released in 1990.

The most remarkable thing about his story is that he was not consumed with anger, hate, or a need for vengeance after he was set free. Instead, he worked with his oppressors to end apartheid, ran for president of South Africa, and led an unparalleled racial reconciliation process.

Earlier in the book, I raised Hannah Arendt's claim that forgiveness is truly the most miraculous aspect of being human. That was certainly the case for Mandela. Seeking revenge would have been most understandable after everything he went through, but he chose to be a unifier instead. He kept his heart open despite a lifetime of adversity. That mindset and the actions it instigated won him the Nobel Peace Prize in 1993.

After his term as president, Mandela kept on combating poverty and HIV/AIDS through his charitable Nelson Mandela Foundation and worked tirelessly on bringing about peace. In a 2002 Newsweek interview he confessed:

"I really wanted to retire and rest and spend more time with my children, my grandchildren and of course with my wife. But the problems are such that for anybody with a conscience who can use whatever influence he may have to try to bring about peace, it's difficult to say no."

Remarkable Role Models

As I have made clear, I do not believe in perfection. That is why I never put people on pedestals and worship them. Yet, I do see people as role models. I see behaviors that can be replicated. That is what Gandhi, Mother Teresa, Williams, and Mandela are to me. Role models. They weren't flawless, yet they stepped into the public square—where everyone gets criticized no matter who they are and what they do—and devoted their lives to caring for others in the best ways they knew how. They showed an ability to stay centered during times of tremendous pressure and overcame periods of grief, doubt and despair with a devotion to causes larger than themselves. Selfish needs were supplanted by selflessness. When they could have stopped, when they could have retired and thought only of themselves, all four continued to work for the benefit of people they did not know because it was the right thing to do.

When I go through difficult days of my own, I often think of them and it helps me get back on track. I try to emulate their admirable actions and forgive them their limitations. It is my sincere hope that you have role models of your own that you can look to for inspiration. Just remember that imitation is preferable to glorification.

Nurturing Seeds of Care and Compassion

Nurturing *basic human decency* and *empathy* has been at the core of all forms of spirituality for millennia. It seems that every religion and moral path has asked adherents to expand their circles of care and develop attitudes of altruism.

It's rather amazing when you think about it. Our collective moral evolution does not seem to have been dependent on a single ideology or mode of thinking but rather bubbled to the surface in all of them. In his classic, *The Varieties of Religious Experience*, William James aptly illustrates that:

"When we survey the whole field of religion, we find a great variety in the thoughts that have prevailed there; but the feelings on the one hand and the conduct on the other are almost always the same, for Stoic, Christian, and Buddhist saints are practically

indistinguishable in their lives. The theories which Religion generates, being thus variable, are secondary; and if you wish to grasp her essence, you must look to the feelings and the conduct as being the more constant elements."

His findings need to be underlined. Saints, people who have diligently marched their chosen path to completion, are almost indistinguishable in their lives. Their traditions diverge, both in thought and content, but the outcomes in behavior are amazingly similar.

As you can imagine, this sort of 'any path will get you there' conclusion doesn't sit well with people who truly believe that theirs is the only right path, but in a religiously pluralistic society, James's conclusions should allay some fears. He is suggesting that the seeds of care and empathy are built into every human being and that a variety of soils and fertilizers will allow those same seeds to grow and flourish.

When people devote themselves to their chosen paths with sincerity and intensity and their next-door neighbors do the same, then everyone should eventually meet at the pinnacle of love and compassion... but it doesn't always happen that way, does it? In fact, rigorous adherence to one path often creates disdain for others. *Why is that?*

The Attraction-Repulsion Principle

Ancient civilizations in the Indus valley made several observations about human nature that still hold true to this day. One of those observations simply states that when an emotional attraction (*raga*) to one thing grows, it creates automatic repulsion (*dvesha*) for the opposite.

In short, our like for one thing, instinctively (and often unconsciously) creates a dislike for another. I call this the *attraction-repulsion principle*.

Take dieting as an example. The more you are attracted to healthy foods, the more unhealthy foods disgust you. It's like stretching a rubber band—the stronger the attraction becomes, the stronger your repulsion. If people are moderately attracted to healthy foods, then they are moderately repulsed by unhealthy foods. But, once people become 'health nuts'—affectionately called so by others who do not share their strong attraction (wink, wink, nudge, nudge)—they condemn all those who have the occasional candy bar, soda, or fast-food meal and continually rail against sugar- and processed food industries as evil.

I quit smoking many years ago by training myself to be repulsed by cigarettes and attracted to my new smoke-free life. Unfortunately, I found myself going too far and ended up being repulsed by smokers, looking down on them and calling them all sorts of names. Upon realizing my mistake, I backed off and started helping people to quit smoking instead, something I did for the following ten years. My initial repulsion had gone too far. I've stayed smoke-free ever since by focusing on the benefits and being mindful of the co-humanity I share with people who still smoke.

Those who have no strong preferences have a difficult time understanding *the attraction-repulsion principle*. 'Why are these people so upset?' they think to themselves and shrug shoulders. 'I don't get it.'

The answer is simple. It's because they [insert any ideological label] fervently believe in the righteousness of their ideas. It is a tendency that is easy to spot among environmentalists, vegans, political activists, humanists, and is found in some shape or form in every single religious or spiritual environment.

Yet, we should not throw stones in glass houses. This tendency exists in seed form within all of us. The stronger our love for something becomes, the easier it is for us to dislike, despise or even hate the opposite. In fact, hate and bigotry are often born of good intentions. Love for a nation can turn into hate for another nation; love for the environment can turn into hate of polluters; love for animals can turn into hate of those who eat them; love for one ideological label can turn into hate for another... and on it goes.

These days, we see this principle very clearly in politics, where people are willing to accuse each other of malevolence just because of differing political ideologies while both sides consider themselves virtuous. The more devoted one side is to their cause, the more they despise the other, which is one reason why extremism is bad for democracy.

Most prominently, though, we see this proclivity in religion. In religion, attraction and repulsion are not merely dependent on personal preferences. Behaviors have been chosen for followers through a combination of religious scriptures and creeds. Devotees are told, in no uncertain terms, what is good and what is evil.

Regrettably, such distinctions don't always age well. Rabbi Jonathan Henry Sacks has pointed out that each of the world's religions includes *"potential minefields"* that need to be weeded out, as many religious scriptures offer strong condemnation of women, homosexuality, certain eating habits, types of clothing, and much more.

Offenses were (and still are in some places) even punishable by death, which shows an exceptionally strong repulsion. Buddhist philosopher Daisaku Ikeda rightly said that:

"Each religion can be made a force for good or for evil by the people who practice it."

Like it or not, this built-in propensity is universal among human beings. It is a principle that shows itself throughout. Workshop attendees have told me stories of how strong emotions for nearly everything, including politics, tribal identity, food, drugs, alcohol, and environmental concerns, to name a few, have generated hostile feelings towards the opposite.

To my surprise, one participant found the attraction-repulsion principle so repugnant that he condemned my whole program because of it. He believed that I was stuck in the wrong paradigm and that we should move beyond such labels of duality. His words were sharp and his indignation was evident to all. Yet, in all honesty, and because this was an online workshop, we weren't sure whether he was cheekily underscoring the principle or if he was firmly against it.

While some may interpret this ancient observation as black and white, *the attraction-*

repulsion principle exists in shades of gray. The correlation is based on the strength of emotion. Once energy is committed in a single ideological direction there is a tendency to dismiss, dislike, and eventually become disgusted by the opposite.

For instance, if someone is a fair weather fan of a sports team, winning and losing means less to him. The stronger the emotional connection becomes, the more the team's successes and failures influence his life, and the more he allows himself to detest the team's opponents. There is a reason why we see a constant emphasis on sportsmanship in student athletics. It's essentially a warning against the natural inclination towards strong repulsion.

To make this principle more complicated, there are *multitudes of interest and ideologies* in life that tug on our emotions. A person can show a moderate temperament in relation to most topics but then show an exceptionally strong belief for or against something, seemingly out of character. When that happens, we often say that we've 'struck a nerve.'

The gist of it is simple. Strong emotions for something can easily turn into negative attitudes towards the opposite. Cultivation of goodness, kindness, and care can turn into a judgment of contrasting behaviors at any time.

My father, rest his soul, always used to say that the stronger the sun is, the stronger the shadow. One cannot exist without the other. It is only when people are made aware of this predisposition that they can reduce its harm.

Karen Armstrong, who established the Charter for Compassion, eloquently wrote that:

"We can either emphasize those aspects of our traditions, religious or secular, that speak of hatred exclusion, and suspicion or work with those that stress the interdependence and equality of all human beings."

In politics, we can either take an anti-approach and rail against those elements in 'the other' that we see as repugnant, indignant, and morally reprehensible or take the pro-approach and describe the kind of world we want to live in, talk about solutions, and envision the kind of society that we can create if we come together.

In religion, we can either emphasize the elements of love, compassion, empathy, peace of mind, and interconnectedness that lead to sainthood, as William James described it, or we can condemn, repudiate, and excommunicate all those who don't follow the rules (as written) to our satisfaction.

Helen Keller described the human fascination with repulsion well when she said:

"It is wonderful how much time good people spend fighting the devil. If they would only expend the same amount of energy loving their fellow men, the devil would die in his own tracks of ennui."

While that is a beautiful sentiment—and, trust me, I have found myself daydreaming about only focusing on the sunlight and dismissing the shadow altogether—it's not quite that simple. Just as there are good elements in every human being that can be nurtured, there are also primal tendencies in all of us that we need to be aware of.

In his book, *The World's Religions*, Huston

Smith pointed out that anthropologists have yet to unearth a type of civilized society that did not place any restrictions on human behavior. Morality presents us with a delicate balancing act.

Moderating Behaviors

Overall, strong emotional attraction has many benefits. Austere adherence to everything from dietary rules to moral principles has been shown to deliver positive results. Strong emotions can fire people up and make the 'e' in emotion stand for energy in motion. Groups of people, who have centered their passions on a single mission, are nearly unstoppable. Unwavering beliefs can move mountains. There is a reason why the magnetic pull of emotional attraction has created so many impassioned believers over the millennia.

However, for the sake of social harmony, people need to keep their love for one thing from turning into hate for another.

That is where moderating behaviors come in. They are not meant to moderate attraction or reduce belief, but rather to lessen the likelihood of repulsive obsession, which is a destructive power that can tear through everything from personal relationships to diplomatic relations. There is a big difference between harboring a mild aversion to something and aggressively waging war against ideas and people we don't like.

Although it is quite impossible to quell the human predisposition for repulsion altogether, especially as emotions grow stronger, we can reduce the potential harm.

Here are five moderating behaviors that have been known to save people from their own worst instincts:

1. **Focus On Attraction**
   Human beings can only hold a limited number of things in their conscious mind at any one time and we should employ that knowledge to our benefit, for example, by focusing more on behaviors and ideologies that attract us, making it so that there is less mental bandwidth left for something else. Instead of railing against hate, we focus on love; instead of judging the angry, we offer them our peaceful presence; instead of warning against a dystopian future, we provide a hopeful vision. Sure, it can be good to be aware of the worst that can happen and be knowledgeable of ideas that are antithetical to harmony, but then it is important to focus on solutions, everything from recognizing co-humanity to learning and sharing through dialogue and developing harmony from within.

2. **Be Aware of this Principle**
   Awareness of *the attraction-repulsion principle* is often enough to moderate the most extreme manifestations. "Whoops. I was so attracted to this idea that I became repulsed by something that didn't use to bother me. Good thing I noticed." This approach is simple enough, but it does require self-reflection.

3. **Develop Humility**
   Humility is advocated in both religion and

science. Everyone who pushes their limits, whether they are mental, emotional, intellectual, or spiritual, will find that the more they know, the more they know they don't know. This understanding should lead to humility. Even if we believe in something with our entire being, humility reminds us that, due to the enormity of the universe, there are still many things that we do not and will never know.

4. Keep Your Sense of Humor

According to research by Dr. Arthur Deikman, religious cults have no sense of humor. Extremism thrives on seriousness. We have to maintain the ability to laugh, especially at our own expense. Laughing diffuses tension and moderates the repulsive disposition.

5. Slow Down to Understand

In his book, *Thinking Fast and Slow*, Daniel Kahneman demonstrates how we use our fast-thinking capacity to navigate the world most of the time. Thinking fast is based on our genetic tendencies (collective lessons from navigating the wild, for example), preferred ideologies (confirmation bias, where we look for evidence to confirm what we already believe), labeling (the terms we use to describe our surroundings), and personal experiences, to name a few. In short, thinking fast is like driving a speedy car. Our field of vision narrows the faster we go. While thinking fast can help us in daily life (which is usually somewhat repetitive) it produces severe limits on our capacity when we are faced with unfamiliar circumstances and are trying to find solutions to new problems. Slowing down the thinking process produces better results in those situations. Harmony in a diverse world relies on a capacity for slowing down, setting aside our preconceived ideas and initial dislikes, and making an effort to understand 'the other' with nuance. The more you know about what people believe, why they believe it, what motivates them as human beings, and so on, the less likely you are to respond to them with antipathy.

Our Remaining Dilemma

Here is a counterpoint. I heard it said the other day that it was better to be passionate about serving thousands of people while being judgmental of those who did not do the same than it was to shrug shoulders and not care either way. I am certainly not advocating for apathy, but I am advocating against extremism, strong repulsion, and hate. Those elements never lead to increased social harmony. Rabbi Abraham Joshua Heschel worded our dilemma well when he said:

"The problem to be faced is: how to combine loyalty to one's own tradition with reverence for different traditions."

In my interfaith endeavors, I have found that underneath the surface is a lingering belief that 'the others' are slightly deluded. Every group of zealous believers inwardly shakes their heads at those who believe differently. 'Surely, they can't believe that,' they think to themselves (and this can also be true when they are looking at people of separate sects in the same religion). Yet, within the interfaith space, believers still mingle, they still tolerate each other, and they still see the humanity they share.

That's the whole point of the exercise.

If moderating behaviors result in tolerance rather than devotees calling for God to punish the infidels, then we are on the right track. If people of different faiths and ideologies can occupy the same space without resorting to name-calling and violence, then we have taken additional steps in the right direction. And if all of that leads to friendships and fellowship down the road, even better, but as I mentioned earlier in the book, don't discount tolerance—it is always better than the opposite.

Expanding the Circle

To summarize what we have covered in this movement, shifting from self-care to world-care is a choice. Those who are willing to grow and actively expand their circle will:

- ✓ Use devotion to their chosen spiritual or humanistic tradition to increase capacity for love, care and compassion
- ✓ Actively empathize by attempting to understand other people's perspectives, even when they don't agree with them
- ✓ Practice moderating behaviors to stave off

natural tendencies towards revulsion that come with increased emotional attraction
- ✓ Beware of the need for perfection, both in themselves and those who they have chosen as their role models
- ✓ Remember that sacrifices represent a personal choice and a willingness to serve

Once people clearly perceive humanity's inter-connectedness and feel an internal need to care for others, even those they don't know, they are moving in the direction of world-care. Thomas Merton, who was an American Trappist monk, explained the internal drive thusly:

"The whole idea of compassion is based on the keen awareness of the interdependence of all these living beings."

* * *

PERSONAL INITIATIVES

Commit to Your Path

To increase your capacity for care, *commit to your path*. If you are a Christian, Muslim or Hindu, then be a better Christian, Muslim or Hindu. If you are a humanist, be a better humanist. If you meditate for peace of mind, devote yourself to your meditation practice. If you serve and volunteer every chance you get, keep doing that with an open heart.

As William James concluded based on his

studies, those who tread their chosen paths to completion will likely meet at the apex of compassion, love, and humility, even if their starting points are different.

Research Your Role Models

If you have role models, research their lives. Read memoirs and autobiographies if available, browse through their Wikipedia pages and watch videos, weigh both the positive aspects of their lives and the critiques leveled against them.

Getting to know the ins and outs of people's lives is important. It gives a nuanced view that is rooted in authentic human complexity.

Interestingly enough, the imperfections we find — so long as they are not disqualifying atrocities (remember to assign good intent and try to see things from the prevailing perspective of each period) — can actually help us move forward and take action. The reasoning is simple: "If such and such did this and that despite his or her imperfections, then I can do it as well."

Practice Moderating Behaviors

You may already have begun appraising your beliefs and values in relation to *the attraction-repulsion principle*. Take it a step further by creating a written list of likes and corresponding dislikes. Once you've uncovered strong aversions (we all have one or two), then make sure you are practicing moderating behaviors for balance. Recall that the goal is not to water down your beliefs, but rather to keep love for one thing from turning into hate for another.

Create a Workable Self-Care Plan

You are worthy of self-care. If you sacrifice everything, there will be nothing left to give. In fact, you will be cheating the people that you are committed to serving. Do the necessary research and create a workable self-care plan for physical, emotional, and mental health to reduce the likelihood of burnout.

CODA: BRIDGING DIVIDES

Overview

- The most important thing about this book is what happens after you read it
- To be a communal bridge-builder, you need to identify chasms, do an inventory of your tools and building blocks, improve your skills, create a blueprint, and start building
- Being the change requires confidence in your ability to solve problems and follow your goals and dreams
- Let us be actively hopeful for the future and keep affirming humanity

During an author workshop I attended ten years ago, Mark Victor Hanson, co-author of the *Chicken Soup for the Soul* series, kept asking people what they thought of as the most important thing about his workshop.

Initially, participants answered by listing all the things they had learned. He responded by saying that it was *none of that*. The most important thing was what would happen when they were back home. It was what they *did* that mattered, not how many interesting notes they had taken.

That was a powerful lesson, one I have never forgotten. An emphasis on action was already incorporated into most of my workshops, lectures, and seminars at the time, but afterward, it became my primary focus. I realized that all my programs were for planning and that performance was the next logical step.

The same is true about the material in this book. Without action, we can relegate ideas about social harmony and bridge-building to the realm of wishful thinking. Correspondingly, the most important question you can ask yourself right now is:

"What am I going to do when I am done reading?"

Moving from inaction to action is no easy task. Despite our best efforts, doubt, fear, and hesitancy are inherent. All human beings tend to second-guess themselves and postpone action.

In the 18th Century, Edmund Burke famously posited that for evil to triumph, all that was needed was for good men to do nothing.

The same can be said about our times. As acrimony gets a tighter grip on democratic society, good people can either sit on the sidelines, debilitated by anxiety and daily distractions, or they can overcome indecision and work towards harmony.

Co-Humanity is the Construction Material

Bridge-builders use shared humanity as construction material to reach across ideological divides. When human connections have been established, people are able to meet in the middle and do their best to sing in harmony with each other. The chorus doesn't need to be perfect (as I keep repeating), it only needs to resonate somewhere on the spectrum between tolerance and friendship. Eboo Patel, who is the founder of Interfaith Youth Core, constantly reminds his trainees that:

"Bridges don't fall from the sky, they don't rise from the ground. People build them."

Bridges are made with intention. They make it possible to go between two places that were previously difficult to access. In the natural world, earthly forces create divides, but in society, ideological divides are manmade. This means that only human beings can bridge the chasms that have been created by human beings.

Checklist for Bridge-Builders

The following is a brief checklist I created for ideological bridge-builders:

✓ **Identify Divides**
Begin by looking around you and list divisions that already exist. It is important to begin close to home and look for divides in your family,

faith community, and neighborhood first, and then expand your field of vision and explore communications between religious groups and detect chasms that exist in race relations, political behaviors, and so on. Once you have a list of identified divides, prioritize them based on a combination of three things; (a) the importance and urgency of bridging the gap, (b) your current skill level, and (c) the most suitable place to start construction. A real-world builder tries to find the best location to bridge a ravine by looking for strong foundations on each side and a narrow gap with easy access. I always suggest to people that they begin with smaller divides closer to home while they train themselves to become better bridge-builders.

✓ **Catalog Your Tools and Building Blocks**
We have explored a variety of tools and building blocks, such as becoming aware of acrimony, focusing on co-humanity (merely using that term can have a positive effect and help people see the elements we all share), strengthening human bonds through experiences, using structured dialogue to frame discussions, and much more.
In addition, you already have access to tools and building blocks that you've gathered through your education and experience. Make an inventory of everything that can be of use to you in your work.

✓ **Develop Your Skills**
Practice is needed on all fronts, from nurturing

harmony from within to dialogue facilitation and beyond. If you are serious, you will make a commitment to continual improvement through repetitive rehearsals.

✓ **Join/Gather a Crew**
Bridges are rarely built single-handedly. Look around and join crews that are already building bridges or gather a team of your own.

✓ **Create a Blueprint**
In the same way that real-world bridge-builders need blueprints to make sturdy constructions, ideological bridge-builders need personal plans of action. Create your blueprint and continually refine it.

✓ **Take Action**
Nothing substitutes action. For things to get done, someone needs to do something. Take the first step, then the next step... and before you know it, something has been done, and you've been a part of doing it.

Confidence to Be the Change

Inner voices of doubt and fear can be powerful detractors. "Who do I think I am?" "What can I possibly give to the world?" "I am so flawed that I can hardly be the change."

To overcome limiting beliefs, we, the aspiring peacemakers and bridge-builders of the world, must find ways to empower ourselves. Thankfully, self-confidence is not static. I can have a lot of self-confidence in one area of my life and little in another. In addition, the feeling can fluctuate from one year to the next, and, since self-confidence can decrease, it can also increase. In the context of social harmony, the goal is not to be better than anyone else, rather to be confident enough to take action. As such, self-confidence can be defined as:

- Confidence to solve problems
- Confidence to work towards goals and dreams

This dual definition subtracts chest thumping and narcissism from self-confidence and replaces it with solution- and action-orientation.

When you think about it, confidence is in many ways synonymous with trust. Do you trust yourself to deal with anything that life can throw at you? If you answer yes, then you can move mountains. If you answer no, you have two choices. You can either give up or rebuild trust in yourself. If you choose the latter, it will take time, just like it would take a while for you to trust a person that betrayed you.

Having said that, you can *start acting as if you have confidence already*. The reason is that while self-confidence is related to your character, education, and experience, it is also based on the *feelings of trust* that you generate from within. Therefore, you can fake it 'till you make it. Walk tall, keep an eye on your goals, start taking action, and then get out of your own way. Repeated actions in spite of doubts will give signals to your subconscious mind and your self-confidence will increase with every step to you take.

If you sense that your confidence is faltering, remember these words spoken by Mother Teresa:

"Not all of us can do great things, but we can do small things with great love."

Ultimately, we need to be willing to overlook non-debilitating flaws when we take action. Perfectionism stops too many people in their tracks. If a flaw is not directly related to your capacity for performing something, feel free to overlook it. Sincerity and authenticity are more important than perfection.

Being Actively Hopeful

The term 'hope' often indicates a passive state of sitting around and waiting for the best. I prefer being actively hopeful—purposely cultivating a sense of harmony within myself and doing my best to influence the outside world. Remember that we only need one or two peacemakers or bridge-builders in every group of 40-120 people for harmony to spread rapidly. Sadly, the same is true of the opposite. It only takes one or two rabble-rousers to incite acrimony, and, to pile it on, negative influences often outweigh positive ones.

That is why we need to redouble our efforts and be actively hopeful. We need to band together through our co-humanity, cultivate a vision of a more harmonious society, and work tirelessly towards its fulfillment. None of that is easy, but we have to believe that it is possible. We need to have faith in our shared vision and be actively hopeful.

Keep Affirming Humanity

An ancient Hindu prayer encourages the believer to lift the veil and see God everywhere. Likewise, we, the willing, should practice the art of lifting the ideological veil and seeing co-humanity everywhere. We must be mindful of all the elements that tie us together. We breathe the same air, drink the same water, and are made of the same stardust. The illusion that we are completely separate is a powerful one. It can only be overcome with intentional awareness. Albert Einstein explained the principle of connection beautifully when he said:

"A human being is a part of the whole called by us the universe, a part limited in time and space. He experiences himself, his thoughts and feelings as something separated from the rest, a kind of optical delusion of his consciousness. This delusion is a kind of prison for us, restricting us to our personal desires and to affection for a few persons nearest to us. Our task must be to free ourselves from this prison by widening our circle of compassion to embrace all living creatures and the whole of nature in its beauty."

Mentally affirming "I see our co-humanity" or "we belong to the same tribe" during human interactions may feel unnatural at first, but with time and practice it will become instinctive. We will not necessarily love or even like every other person, but affirming co-humanity will help us experience how all of us are connected, which, in turn, will influence how we act.

Let Us Work Together...

The tools, ideas, and time-tested strategies that I've provided in this book are waiting to be put to good use. Please, stay in touch and keep me informed about the impact of your efforts. For now, allow me to bid you farewell with the following words:

I see you, human being
I thank you for reading
Let us be reminded that we are all connected
Let us work together towards harmony

Rev. Gudjon Bergmann
Harmony Interfaith Initiative
www.harmonyii.org

* * *

PERSONAL INITIATIVES

Develop Your Personal Plan

Develop your personal plan by answering the following open-ended questions. Approach the task like a brainstorming exercise and write everything that comes to mind in response to each question.

You may want to scroll through your notes and explore the resource section at the back of this book before you begin. Don't stop writing until you've entirely drained your well of ideas.

1. What do you want to do (list everything that comes to mind)?
2. Which tools/ideas/strategies/building blocks are you going to use?
3. When do you want to get started?
4. Why do you want to do it (what is your motivation, go deep)?
5. Who can help you or work with you?
6. How will you motivate your crew/team?
7. Where will you launch your efforts or lend a hand?
8. How will you spread the word?

Additional questions:

1. What (if anything) is stopping you?
2. What do you need to improve to be able to do what you have planned?

Your answers to these—and other questions that will pop up as you write—will generate a blueprint that you can continually refine.

The personal action plan will allow you to build a strong foundation on your side of the chasm and then reach across to see if you can find willing co-operators on the other side.

While a clear written plan may not work out exactly the way you want it to, it will get you started. Once you are moving in the right direction, it is my experience that unexpected doors will open up for you.

Use Harmony Affirmations

Affirmations are first-person present tense statements that influence both conscious and unconscious awareness. Reading affirmations silently or even chanting them aloud can help the mind focus in a specific direction, occupy mental bandwidth, and create a subconscious undercurrent. The following are sample affirmations based on the content in this book.

- I recognize co-humanity in everyone I encounter
- I build bridges across divides
- I collaborate with other bridge-builders
- I seek peace through understanding
- I choose strategies over platitudes
- If people dehumanize, I re-humanize
- I nurture harmony from within
- I dialogue to learn, share and create trust
- I honor diversity and celebrate similarities
- I create harmony in my corner of the world
- My thoughts are seeds, my words are water, my actions are soil, I nurture harmony
- I play a harmonious role in the human orchestra
- In the global village, everyone is my neighbor
- Humanity is my tribe

VARIATIONS: WHAT BRIDGE-BUILDERS SAY ABOUT HARMONY

Overview

- This addendum provides a variety of perspectives
- Nineteen people offer their views on social harmony and bridge-building

Most people are familiar with the parable of the three blind men who were attempting to describe an elephant. One held the trunk, another the tail, and the third held the belly while they argued vehemently about which one of them was right in their description of the elephant. In their own way, they were all correct. Each held a vital piece of the puzzle. Ken Wilber articulates this idea of multiple perspectives well:

"I have one major rule: Everybody is right. More specifically, everybody—including me—has some important pieces of truth, and all of those pieces need to be honored, cherished, and included in a more gracious, spacious, and compassionate embrace. To Freudians I say, Have you looked at Buddhism? To Buddhists I say, Have you studied Freud? To liberals I say, Have you thought about how important some conservative ideas are? To conservatives I say, Can you perhaps include a more liberal perspective? And so on, and so on, and so on... At no point have I ever said: Freud is wrong, Buddha is wrong, liberals are wrong, conservatives are wrong. I have only suggested that they are true but partial. My critical writings have never attacked the central beliefs of any discipline, only the claims that the particular discipline has the only truth—and on those grounds I have often been harsh. But every approach, I honestly believe, is essentially true but partial, true but partial, true but partial. And on my own tombstone, I dearly hope that someday they will write: He was true but partial..."

True but partial is a statement that I resonate with deeply. It describes my efforts in a nutshell. That is why I sought input from a range of people in this addendum. I wanted to give you an opportunity to explore the core concepts of social harmony and bridge-building from a variety of angles, to see viewpoints and dimensions that I had not adequately covered.

Three Questions, Nineteen Answers

In late August and early September 2018, I sent

out a questionnaire and gave the recipients two months to ponder their answers. Some responded quickly while others took their time. Some answers were short while others were long. I got nineteen responses overall, which means that on the following pages you will find nineteen answers to the same three questions. The quality of responses way exceeded what I had dared to hope. Every person, who graciously accepted my invitation to participate in this project, is highly qualified in his or her field. From doctors and reverends to business people and psychologists, the breadth and width of perspectives is truly astounding.

The Contributors and their Organizations

I urge you to take time to get to know all the contributors and the organizations that they represent. Look at their websites and explore their work. If you like what you see, please share their work through your social media channels. All of them are making a positive difference in the world and should be celebrated.

Here is a list of all nineteen:

- Yehuda Stolov (p. 151)
  Interfaith Encounter Association
- Sari Heidenreich (p. 156)
  United Religions Initiative
- Rabbi Jack Moline (p. 158)
  Interfaith Alliance
- Marilyn Turkovich (p. 161)
  Charter for Compassion

Note that I did not want other perspectives to bleed into my writings and did not read any of the answers until after I had finished writing the book. The parallels you'll see have arisen naturally and without any coordination.

* * *

Yehuda Stolov
Interfaith Encounter Association

1. How do you define social harmony?

Social harmony is a reality in which peoples' and communities' lives are guided by the awareness that we all coexist as different organs in the same body or different flowers in the same garden. Therefore they care for each other and work together to support the well being of all. They understand that an approach of competition leads to waste of energy and resources, therefore less beneficial even for the winning side.

In the reality of social harmony people still hold different points of view on many issues and may still have contradicting interests, but they understand that each view adds its unique perspective and enriches our knowledge of the issue. They understand that the best way for them is to reconcile the contradiction of interests through jointly finding the way that will maximize the benefits of all sides. They do not see this as a compromise because they care not only for themselves but also for the others.

2. What is the best bridge-building technique you have come across or used?

When we analyze the disapproving attitudes that many in our communities have for each other we realize that these are not the result of an educated decision that it is impossible to live together. On the contrary: negative attitudes result from the generalization of individual cases of negativity, which creates prejudices and off-putting stereotypes that result in a negative image of the 'other.'

The problem with such images is that they are psychologically rooted and it is not enough to explain the actual reality to counteract them. To uproot them we need an experience that will be psychologically significant. The interfaith encounter in which participants truly and deeply meet the 'other' face-to-face, provides such an experience and can be profoundly transformative.

Interfaith encounter focuses on themes that relate to the foundation of the respective cultures and touches on issues that have deep existential meaning for the participants, even for the most secular among them. Discussing together how one relates to religion and religious texts and ideas allows us to address core issues of identity and meaning and to find shared values. The discussion becomes much more intimate than just an exchange of opinions and gives room for the exposure of the humanity of the 'other,' which happens when people really look into each other's eyes. Moreover, this focus reveals large degrees of similarities between participants' traditions. This idea of discovering shared values may sound pedestrian but can be a tremendous revelation for participants. Finally, this angle allows for a constructive way to discuss differences. In this way, participants train themselves to develop friendships with people they disagree with, which is the real challenge we face.

Consequently, an interfaith encounter is not only relevant for those who enjoy interfaith dialogue or learning for their own sake. Interfaith encounters are important for any person who lives in a split society, as it gives ordinary people an avenue to make an actual contribution towards real peace — directly, without being dependent on their leaders. Knowing and understanding the 'other' directly, in turn, alleviates the fear from all members of their community and thus improves the quality of life for participants.

An interfaith encounter is a meaningful conversation in which participants exchange ideas on issues that have existential significance for them, and consequently get to know one another in a more intimate way. It reveals similarities and helps build bridges between people. At the same time, it enables people to share their differences in a constructive, respectful way, which allows the conversation to proceed and indeed deepen without defensiveness or anyone feeling threatened. In this way, interfaith encounter enables its participants to develop friendships with those they disagree with and had even been in fear of previously; this of course is the real challenge of peacebuilding in the Holy Land.

The most common way to conduct an interfaith encounter is through joint learning of our respective religions, traditions, and cultures. In the Holy Land, these carry existential meaning for everyone and can be used to connect any group of people. However, other platforms of in-depth exchange may work better for specific groups of people: music, literature, shared vocation or interest, etc. Through the transformative power of interfaith encounter, people abandon the prejudices and stereotypes they hold of each other, replacing them with a direct and real understanding that leads to respect, trust, and friendship.

3. What does your organization do to promote social harmony?

The Interfaith Encounter Association (IEA) works to promote genuine coexistence and sustainable peace, through joint community building on the grassroots level, using interactive interfaith dialogue as its vehicle. The apolitical and all-inclusive approach of the organization and its activities enable the successful participation of a very wide range of participants and thus to continuously build a true grassroots movement which constitutes the human infrastructure for peace in the Holy Land.

In its seventeen years of existence, the IEA has held—within Israel, between Israelis and Palestinians and in the larger Middle East—more than 2,700 programs, with many thousands of participants. A most significant fact is that the participants in IEA programs include people of all political and religious views, as well as all ages, genders, walks of life, etc.; and that the vast majority of them have met 'the other' for the first time through IEA. As of this date, the IEA has founded 98 ongoing community-groups of interfaith encounter – from the Upper Galilee to Eilat, including 36 groups that bring together on a regular basis Israelis and West Bank Palestinians.

More can be found at:
www.interfaith-encounter.org

Biography

Yehuda Stolov is the executive director of the Interfaith Encounter Association, an organization that works since 2001 to build peaceful inter-communal relations in the Holy Land by fostering mutual respect and trust between people and communities through active interfaith dialogue. Dr. Stolov has lectured on the role of religious dialogue in peace building throughout the world, including Jordan, India, Indonesia, Turkey, South Korea, North America, and Europe. He also published many papers on related issues. In 2006, he was awarded the Immortal Chaplains Foundation Prize for Humanity, which honors those who "risked all to protect others of a different faith or ethnic origin"; and in 2015 he was awarded the IIE Victor J. Goldberg Prize for Peace in the Middle East. Among other activities, Dr. Stolov is a member of the International Council of the International Association for Religious Freedom and was a member of the steering committee for the United Nations Decade of Interreligious Dialogue and Cooperation for Peace. He holds a B.Sc. and an M.Sc. in Physics and a

Ph.D. from the Hebrew University of Jerusalem.
He is married and father of three children, living in
Jerusalem.

Sari Heidenreich
United Religions Initiative

1. How do you define social harmony?

To me, the term social harmony immediately
makes me think of music, which is something I
dearly love. When people harmonize while
singing a song, they are singing different parts of
the same chord. I think this is a beautiful metaphor
for what harmony can look like in society—
different people, singing different notes but to the
same tune. Practically, this means that we do not
all need to look the same, or sound the same and
that, in fact, the ways in which we sound or look
different make our community more complex and
more beautiful.

2. What is the best bridge-building technique you have come across or used?

This may seem simple, but the technique that
I have seen work time and time again, in a variety
of places around the globe, is bringing people
together to serve in their community. The act of
serving side-by-side with someone is an intensely
bonding experience, one that helps you see that,
no matter what else you might not agree on, you
do agree on something -- the value of this project.
So, whether it be a construction project, a park

clean-up, building toilets, providing disaster relief, or any number of other things, if you have a group of people that you need to bring into positive contact with one another — get them serving together!

3. What does your organization do to promote social harmony?

The United Religions Initiative is a network of nearly 1,000 groups in more than 100 countries who have come together because of a common purpose: to promote daily, enduring interfaith cooperation, to end religiously motivated violence and to create cultures of peace, justice, and healing for the earth and all living being. Each of these groups is made up of at least seven people from at least three different religions, spiritual expressions or indigenous traditions. They all operate independently but interact with the URI network in order to share best practices, get connected to resources and build collective impact. URI believes that, by uniting people doing similar work with similar values, we can build collective impact and create a global movement of people. Specifically, URI does this by providing the framework for people to build relationships across religious and/or cultural divides, by facilitating meetings and trainings in areas that our members request and by hosting communications platforms for activists from all over the world to connect with one another.

Learn more at:
www.uri.org

Biography

Sari Heidenreich is the North American Regional Coordinator for United Religions Initiative, the world's largest grassroots interfaith peacebuilding network. In this role, Sari supports, connects and empowers grassroots organizers in over 100 interfaith organizations across the U.S. and Canada. Sari spent middle and high school in Ghana, West Africa and as an adult, she has spent time living, traveling and working in the Middle East, including a yearlong stint in Jerusalem.

Rabbi Jack Moline
Interfaith Alliance

1. How do you define social harmony?

Social harmony is the capacity of participants in a community of any size to act together for the common good, preserving the ability of individuals to behave in a way that reflects their values and preferences. Since conflict between the two is inevitable, especially as the size of the community increases, the tolerance for dissonance must eventually be defined, ideally by voluntary cooperation but, if necessary, by rule of law.

2. What is the best bridge-building technique you have come across or used?

Listening is the best technique for bridge-building. It is the behavior that best models humility (which is not thinking less of yourself but thinking of yourself less). True listening involves the ability to restate what another is saying, not manipulating what you hear to give yourself an opening to outdo another.

3. What does your organization do to promote social harmony?

If I am going to be honest, we try to model two paradoxical sets of behavior.

First, we are very careful (I hope) to listen to our opponents and allies and distill from them what is important to them. We then process it in the context of our values, which we identify with both the phenomenon of faith/conscience and the requirements of our Constitutional society.

Second, we are diligent (I hope) in protecting the faith and freedom of all citizens. Whether a theist or a secularist, a Democrat or a Republican, a conservative or a liberal, every person has equal rights and protections under the law. No person's personal convictions exempt that individual from the law nor may they be invoked to deny any other person of those same rights and protections. We are a nation of laws and a people who, out of the many, are one.

Biography

Jack Moline is President of Interfaith Alliance. In a career spanning four decades, he has established himself as a powerful voice fighting for religious freedom for all Americans, regardless of their faith or belief system. As a rabbi, he has worked to create common ground between people of diverse religious and secular backgrounds. As an advocate, he has led efforts to secure services for this disabled, increase the supply of affordable housing, promote marriage equality, ensure pay equity and especially, protect civil rights for people of all faiths and sexual orientations. A native of Chicago, he holds the title of Rabbi Emeritus of Agudas Achim Congregation in Alexandria, Virginia, where he served for 27 years. Rabbi Moline is an adjunct faculty member of the Jewish Theological Seminary and the Virginia Theological Seminary, educating future leaders in the Jewish, Christian and Muslim faith communities. A longtime board member of Interfaith Alliance, serving as chair of the board from 2006-2008, Rabbi Moline has a wealth of experience in interfaith advocacy. He has served as chair of the Interfaith Relations Committee of the Jewish Council for Public Affairs, vice president of the Washington-Baltimore Rabbinical Assembly and board member of the Faith and Politics Institute. He serves on the advisory boards of Clergy Beyond Borders and Operation Understanding DC. He also served as the first director of public policy for the Rabbinical Assembly and was executive director of NJDC. Rabbi Moline is a graduate of Northwestern University. He was ordained by the Jewish Theological Seminary in 1982 from which he received an honorary doctorate in 2012. Rabbi Moline is a long-suffering (and recently redeemed) supporter of the Chicago Cubs. He lives in Alexandria, VA with his wife of 40 years. He is the father of three grown children and proud grandfather of two.

Marilyn Turkovich
Charter for Compassion

1. How do you define social harmony?

"Story is the shortest distance between people."
– Pat Speight

I grew up in a small town in Pennsylvania that was next to another smaller town that was settled by the Harmony Society. Historically the group has been referred to as the Harmonists and it originated in Germany, prior to their coming to the United States, around the early eighteen hundreds. They were an inventive and prosperous group, who adhered to principles that mirrored similar societies of the time; holding property in common and accepting no pay for their work, in return receiving care for their services. They lived simply, but under strict religious doctrine, including advocating celibacy—a quick way to bring the community to an end. I was fascinated by how they lived, worked, worshipped and celebrated together. In some ways it wasn't so different from what I experienced growing up.

As a high school student I would often visit Harmony, it was in the same town as my school. There was something behind those white picket fences that was so appealing and calming. I was drawn to the simplicity and the feel of the place. Don't get me wrong, it was massive, the buildings were generous in size, to a certain extent even industrial in nature, but nonetheless, inviting. I became fascinated with how the group lived in a community. I put my imagination to work. After all, my family was relatively new to this county and stuck close to other Croatians in our town.

How were we different from the Harmonists? My immediate family was an extended family, several of my aunts and uncles living only a block away or in my grandparents' house. My two aunts who lived away from the immediate family, would every weekend make their pilgrimage back to us with their husbands and children in tow. Saturdays were the highlight of the weekends when we all went to the Croatian picnic grounds to experience a gathering of our tribe—an extravaganza that started at lunchtime and ended in the wee hours. Negotiations took place here, food and drink were shared, and music and dancing seemed to validate the gathering.

However, it was the stories that were told of the "old country" that became the glue that bound us together. We did not spend much time beyond our ethnic group, though our physically close Greek and Lebanese neighbors were welcome in our immediate circle.

As I look back on those years, I am convinced that I felt safe in this social group, perhaps the way in which the Harmonists did in their community. I realize now that this sense of safety also evoked a sense of belonging. What could reflect social harmony more than this? However, we were very different from the Harmonists. Something very important occurred in our seemingly close-knit circle and that was that it was not closed to others. In my experience, family or group didn't have to only involve blood relatives or cultural sameness. The ticket to getting into our group was knowing a person's story.

2. What is the best bridge-building technique you have experienced or used?

Consequently, I am convinced that telling our stories is the best bridge-building technique that can be used in getting individuals of different ages, races and ethnic backgrounds together. I remember many decades ago listening to a lecture by the famed psychologist Carl Rogers. He talked about the work he was doing among a group of people from Northern Ireland and the Republic of Ireland. In sharing their stories they affirmed what Plato told us, and I paraphrase here: "be open to others because they too may be suffering just as you are."

There is an approach I have used for years that I learned from Roberto Chene, a proponent of re-evaluation counseling. In a fifteen minute period you can invite two people, who don't necessarily know one another to come together and observe a few rules: listen unconditionally to the other, don't ask questions, respect each other's privacy and keep what you have heard to yourselves. Allow the first person to speak for 5 minutes telling the highlights of their life story — revealing what have been the milestones in his/her life and the other person just listening — no questions, no gestures, just pure presence gifted to the speaker. Switch roles. Same rules. Finally, allow for shared talking. Most often, without retelling stories, the collective analysis reveals the similarities of our life experiences. There are other questions to pursue in the use of re-evaluation counseling and each brings in more depth, understanding, and acceptance of the other, and even acknowledges and appreciates the "other" who may eventually become a part of "one's own" family.

3. What does your organization do to promote social harmony?

We talk. We listen. We invite comment and criticism. We make a sincere effort to be transparent. We frequently fall down after making mistakes, but we work towards resiliency and harmony. The Charter for Compassion is a large organization that exists in more than four hundred cities worldwide, in more than fifty countries, and that has a central database with well over 150,000 members. Our organizational structure is relatively flat, enabling each compassionate initiative in a city to form its own vision statement and come together in community to decide how they will make their city or town a more comfortable place in which to live. They articulate their own concerns, create sustainable action plans, and work to alleviate the suffering in their community. At the base of this sharing is an adherence to the Charter for Compassion, which we can sum up in these few tenants:

- We believe that a compassionate world is possible when every man, woman, and child treats others as they wish to be treated--with dignity, equity, and respect.
- We believe that all human beings are born with the capacity for compassion and that

it must be cultivated for human beings to survive and thrive.

- We know that we can collectively overcome the challenges that we face as a global community.

The Charter for Compassion reflects the Harmonists who planted their roots in a new country in one major way—we seek a harmony that compassionately works for a world at peace.

Biography

Marilyn Turkovich's work has been primarily in areas of global awareness, international education, race and social justice and in instructional design. She has worked internationally in Brazil, Croatia, Guatemala, India and Japan and with community groups in the USA in developing new program approaches in community involvement, action and education. In instructional design, her work includes the authoring or co-authoring of more than twenty-five training and curriculum books and the design of education manuals for development houses and publishing companies. Work on leadership, management skills, change and chaos theory, future thinking, strategic planning and visioning, team building, measurement, communications and diversity awareness, health issues, engineering and law topics, problem solving has been designed for a number of diverse clients.

Marilyn has also been involved in helping a number of public departments and private organizations write strategic, business, development and succession plans. In addition, she has designed a number of training initiatives, including the design of corporate universities (i.e., IBM, Medtronics, City of Seattle—DPD), the writing of content material and instructional training/education programs to be used for training and interactive media and led internationalizing the curriculum projects in a number of colleges and universities (i.e., Colorado College, Columbia College—Chicago, St. Olaf, St. Thomas, Sterling Community College). She has also been involved in education as a teacher, curriculum coordinator, principal and director of a teacher-training program for the Associated Colleges and Columbia College—Chicago for all of her professional life. Currently she is director of the Charter of Compassion International.

Rev. Dirk Ficca
Twin Cities Social Cohesion Initiative

1. How do you define social harmony?

Social harmony can be a fuzzy, elusive and highly subjective concept. Rather than use principles or sociological categories to describe it, I've been drawn to the following questions:

- Are we willing to stand with others—and others with us—in times of need, distress, conflict, loss, and tragedy?
- Have we accompanied another person or a community through times of discovery, struggle, challenge, suffering?

- Are commonly held cultural beliefs or public perceptions of an 'other' countered by a personal relationship or experience?
- Are there other reasons to stay 'at the table' when we disagree with, or disappoint, each other?
- Does the 'common good' play a decisive role in considerations among competing interests?
- Do those impacted or served have 'a seat at the table' and a definitive role in decision-making? Especially the marginalized and those closest to the grassroots?

To the degree we can answer any or all of the questions with 'yes' – and all that has to happen in order to do so – suggests a similar degree of social harmony.

2. What is the best bridge-building technique you have come across or used?

In general, it's all about relationships and their humanizing character. So the short answer is: Get as many people and communities face-to-face with each other as possible—preferably across divides—for positive encounters and constructive conversations. To flesh that out a bit, I can further suggest:

- Begin by understanding and respecting people for who they are - their experience, perspective, needs, aspirations, and motivations.

- Reach out to those still making up their minds about 'who's in' and 'who's out.'
- Do everything through partnership.
- Provide safe environments and inclusive processes for those impacted to share their concerns and aspirations, and to have a decisive role in decision-making.
- Infuse the public discourse with positive images and constructive rhetoric.

3. What does your organization do to promote social harmony?

The Twin Cities Social Cohesion Initiative seeks to build social harmony in the Minneapolis – St. Paul metropolitan area. The Initiative uses an asset-based approach, drawing on all sectors of society – government, business, education, media, the arts, organizations of civil society, and religious and spiritual communities – seeking "...to create a reservoir of trust, goodwill and resilience, so as to meet the practical challenges of living together with mutual respect and shared responsibility."

Through hundreds of appreciative inquiry interviews and reference group conversations, the Initiative learns about the perspective and interest of persons across the societal spectrum about the need for greater social cohesion, and the various paths toward it. Communities that would not otherwise come into contact with each other meet in carefully designed encounters to become aware of preconceptions and promote understanding. Special attention is paid to 'what's working' when it comes to weaving the fabric of the wider populous. Out of these explorations, collaboration and partnerships emerge to address the practical concerns that need to be addressed.

Given that the Twin Cities is a microcosm of the world — of its diversity and its challenges — if it can happen here, it can happen anywhere.

Biography

Rev. Dirk Ficca is currently serving as the Executive Director of the Twin Cities Social Cohesion Initiative in Minneapolis – St. Paul. He is also serving as a senior advisor to the Church of Sweden and its Archbishop for the 'A World of Neighbors' initiative addressing the refugee and migrant crisis in Europe.

From 1992 to 2012, Dirk worked in various capacities with the Council for a Parliament of the World's Religions, serving as Executive Director for the last fifteen years. During his tenure, the Council organized the world's largest international interreligious gatherings, with major Parliament events in Chicago (1993), Cape Town (1999), Barcelona (2004) and Melbourne (2009). Under his leadership, the Council's mission promoted interreligious dialogue, grassroots organizing, and global networking in cities around the world. Dirk received his Master of Divinity from McCormick Theological Seminary in 1981, and served as pastor of the First Presbyterian Church of Benton Harbor, Michigan, for 11 years. He lives in Oak Park, Illinois with his wife Lynda, and two sons Dillon and Connor.

Beth A. Broadway
InterFaith Works of Central New York

1. How do you define social harmony?

When people, often strangers, can come together for a sustained discussion of difficult topics, such as racism and poverty, with empathy and caring to promote more just, equitable and democratic outcomes in our communities. That nonviolent conflict of ideas is necessary for personal and community growth. Those different perspectives, even ones that we do not agree with, do not represent the person. That the web of humanity is comprised of complex individuals. Harmony is not the achievement of everyone singing the same note, but true harmony is achieved by an array of different notes sung together.

2. What is the best bridge-building technique you have come across or used?

InterFaith Works views "dialogue" as an inclusive, strategic process; hence, dialogue is a facilitated, multi-session discussion that has the potential to build trust, respect, and understanding among diverse groups of people. The ability to come together and find common ground on which to stand and a means to move forward on critical social issues even when there is disagreement is part and parcel of dialogue. A "dialogue circle" refers to the group of people that participate in a dialogue over 4-6 sessions of 2 hours per session.

Dialogue circle meetings are facilitated by two trained co-facilitators who have different identities from one another (i.e., ideally they will represent different genders and ethnicities) and are reflective of the group's participants. Dialogue facilitators have experience in both the topic under discussion and with group leadership.

Facilitators use discussion guides that are designed to build relationships among the group and to discuss specific areas of concern, such as racism, interfaith relations, workplace tensions or other forms of stereotyping. The content of these guides serve as meeting agendas and reading sources to focus the dialogue. An initial step in the dialogue process is that participants develop ground rules for how they will talk with one another in the group setting. Specific exercises are used to encourage and elicit discussion. One such exercise allows participants to get to know one another personally, discuss perspectives and solutions relative to topical areas. The end goal remains identification of strategies for commitments to personal and community actions.

A key assumption about dialogue circles is that participants should be ready to listen and learn from others in the group. Other assumptions typically include:

- To identify and to understand the impact of stereotypes, bias, and racism in our culture at both personal and structural levels;
- To develop the understanding and skills necessary for sustained dialogue regarding sensitive issues;

- To cultivate new relationships and friendships;
- To envision a future that provides justice and opportunity for all on many levels: personal, social, educational, economic and political; and
- To recognize that community members often do not have an opportunity for honest and open discussion about difficult topics in a safe space.

3. What does your organization do to promote social harmony?

Founded in 1976, InterFaith Works was born out of the United States Civil Rights Movement by a formidable group of Central New York civil rights and faith leaders to focus on advancing interracial understanding. The agency was progressive in working toward interreligious understanding, as well, first among Jews, Catholics, and Protestants, and then expanding to include Muslims, Sikhs, Mormons, Baha'is, and other faith groups.

Led by an interfaith and multiethnic Board of Directors and Round Table of Faith Leaders, InterFaith Works embraces different faith communities and the region's diverse people to address deeply embedded social divisions and to help the community find common ground on its issues. The agency strives to provide life-changing experiences that lead to the creation of a more equitable and loving community. InterFaith Works social service programs address the needs of and empower people who are vulnerable, low income and targets of oppression, including refugees, the elderly and the institutionalized, through direct service and educational programs. InterFaith Works is committed to the belief that all people are deserving of dignity and respect regardless of ethnicity, faith tradition or social circumstances. Using the tools of deliberative democracy and cross-cultural dialogue, InterFaith Works also addresses deeply embedded social divisions leading to community action and policy change.

Our work is carried out by 32 staff members who are as diverse as those we serve and the Central New York community at large. Sixteen of our staff members are of the global majority, including Middle Eastern, African, Asian, African-American, and Latino.

The agency serves people of diverse races, ethnicities, faiths, ages, educational and socioeconomic backgrounds, gender and sexual orientation through its four main programs: the El-Hindi Center for Dialogue, Interfaith Initiatives, Senior Services and Center for New Americans. The two programs most closely associated with promoting social harmony are the El-Hindi Center for Dialogue and Interfaith Initiatives.

The El-Hindi Center for Dialogue serves as a regional hub for constructive community discussion and dialogue-to-action programs. Its programs bring disparate groups together to foster mutual understanding and trust, and to find ways to work together for the betterment of the whole community. The Center for Dialogue incorporates the ongoing work of the Community Wide

Dialogue to End Racism—now the longest running dialogue of its kind in the nation. Since 1995, more than 15,000 people have participated in more than 600 dialogue circles. Programs within the Center for Dialogue serve those of varying socioeconomic backgrounds, ages, faiths, and ethnicities. Each year, about 1,300 people participate in its programming, which includes:

- The Community Wide Dialogue to End Racism has engaged our community in a structured, 20-plus year community organizing effort about racism, race relations and healing. Each racially mixed dialogue group of eight to 12 people meets for six, two-hour sessions. Two trained and diverse facilitators help the groups work toward a productive discussion in an environment of respect and honesty. Dialogue circles help participants to:
    - explore how racism has affected us
    - uncover stereotypes that need to be challenged
    - understand the differences between personal bigotries and structural racism
    - deepen their commitment to becoming allies and
    - take action in our homes, communities, and workplace
- Police-Community Dialogues seek to build trust, respect, and understanding between groups of people that do not ordinarily have positive interactions. They are informed by the historic, unequal treatment in all aspects of the

criminal justice system, mistrust due to police non-response in neighborhoods, and refugees' experience with police in their home countries and in current investigations combined against the national backdrop of racial profiling and police-civilian shootings.

- Interfaith Dialogues address the challenge of building peace by promoting acceptance of religious and cultural differences to build bridges and eliminate hatred and suspicion. Each group of six to 10 people of diverse spiritual and religious traditions, meets for six, two-hour sessions, led by two diverse co-facilitators. InterFaith Works' dialogue guide is entitled Seeking Common Ground and was informed by a national dialogue model developed by Everyday Democracy.

- The Starting Small Program involves semester-long "exchanges" between suburban and urban school students. The Center for Dialogue uses a facilitated dialogue process, discussion guides and interactive activities to spark conversations, diffuse tensions, break down stereotypes and build bridges of understanding among participating youth. The program serves approximately 350 youth and teens from 14 area schools each academic school year.

- Syracuse Seeds of Peace is a collaborative project initiated with the support of Say Yes to Education, Inc., and sustained through a partnership between InterFaith Works, the Syracuse City School District, Onondaga County, and the national Seeds of Peace organization. The program brings refugee and American born city high school students together to build strategic relationships, and to facilitate deeper understanding, acceptance, and tolerance. The program has brought almost 120 Syracuse City School District students to Otisfield, Maine, to attend the Seeds of Peace Camp for 14 days. While there, youth engage in facilitated dialogue sessions to explore racial identity and to learn how to reduce racially motivated bullying in their schools and communities. These students then support Syracuse Seeds of Peace clubs in each of the five Syracuse high schools to develop peace-building projects in their schools, in partnership with other schools, and in the community.

- Study Circles on Community Issues use a deliberative, democratic process successfully implemented across the United States and globally. Community members engage in discussions about complex social issues and community problems that have multiple potential solutions. Trained facilitators use a carefully crafted, neutral dialogue guide that:
  - describes the issue
  - offers a variety of solutions that represent distinctly different viewpoints
  - lays out the pros and cons of choosing one solution over another
  - presents a set of questions that helps the participants find common ground upon which to craft the solution that the majority of the community can support.

- facilitators help participants clarify their own points of view and listen to points of view that are different from their own. Study Circles occur in multiple locations simultaneously or within a short duration of time and include participants from diverse socioeconomic and ethnic backgrounds. The Dialogues end with an Action Forum that:
- allows the whole community to hear the voices of each group
- further explores the issue through expert panel discussions or additional dialogue circles
- identifies places of community consensus and community division
- creates a space for citizens and community leaders to develop Action Teams to continue the work on addressing the community's issue.

Interfaith Initiatives seeks to increase interfaith understanding among members of various faith traditions and the community at large. To that end, it organizes interfaith events and dialogue programs, working closely with InterFaith Works' more than 60 Faith Partners and its Round Table of Faith Leaders. Interfaith Initiatives also provides spiritual care and religious services to 2,000 people each month who are institutionalized in hospitals, nursing homes, and correctional facilities and who are in need of spiritual and emotional support. The program coordinates the "CNY Inspirations" column that appears in the Syracuse Post-Standard and on Syracuse.com, and events, including the annual World Interfaith Harmony Assembly that highlights the commonalities among all faith traditions and builds understanding, as well as the Spirit of America project that aims to build understanding among of the broader community of issues facing refugees and the refugee resettlement process.

The agencies other programs are:

The Center for New Americans, established in 1981, resettles refugees who have fled war, persecution and natural disaster in some of the most troubled places on earth. Historically, the program has resettled between 300 and 600 refugees each year. The center also provides crucial post-settlement services for up to five years to help refugees re-establish their lives and overcome the barriers necessary for successful integration in the U.S. These services include literacy, employment, housing, referral to medical care, and citizenship preparation. Syracuse is the second largest refugee resettlement city in New York state.

Senior Services coordinates the Senior Companion Program, which provides companionship and advocacy to frail seniors living in Onondaga, Cayuga, and Madison counties. It is a free program serving 180 clients weekly and helps to keep these vulnerable elders socially engaged and living independently in their own homes. In 2018, Senior Services launched the One to One Program, a volunteer-based program providing friendship to "elder orphans" in nursing homes who have no regular visitors.

Biography

For more than 40 years, Beth A. Broadway, M.S Ed., has been a force for justice, raising voice to issues of oppression, and advancing racial and social equity through the process of dialogue and action. Broadway has served as the president/CEO of InterFaith Works since 2010. As CEO, she leads the 501(c)(3) human services agency as it addresses the social service and social justice needs of the Central New York community, with an emphasis on the city of Syracuse. As CEO, she is responsible for leading the financial, management, fundraising, board development and outreach for the $3 million agency.

Throughout her 20-plus year career at InterFaith Works, Broadway has been a champion for those who are vulnerable, low income and targets of oppression. She has used her administrative and hands-on skills to develop programming that builds bridges across community divides that include ethnicity, race, faith, and socioeconomic backgrounds. She successfully has worked to elevate the voices of those who often go unheard and to teach and nurture leadership skills in those who are frequently marginalized.

Prior to becoming CEO of InterFaith Works, she led the Community Wide Dialogue to End Racism (CWD), a program of InterFaith Works. CWD works in grammar schools, middle schools, high schools and with adults to break down stereotypes, build solid relationships, and address the systemic problem of racism in our community. CWD is one of the longest continually running programs of its type in the nation and has touched the lives of more than 12,000 people since its founding. Broadway has been active with the program since it started in 1995, and was the director for nine years. The dialogue programs founded and inspired by Broadway continue to adapt and expand under her leadership to address new community concerns. Recent developments include an Interfaith Dialogue program, a Police-Community Dialogue program, and community dialogues to address Islamophobia following the September 11 attack (and which continue to the present) and most recently Columbus Day and the suggested removal of a statue in his honor that has stood in the heart of Syracuse for eight decades.

In addition to her administrative role at InterFaith Works, Broadway was the designer and facilitator of The Leadership Classroom, now in its 25th year as a project of the Central New York Community Foundation. The initiative provides training and equips grassroots neighborhood leaders to develop projects that improve city neighborhoods and engage neighborhood residents in their community. More than 250 groups have been trained since the Leadership Classroom began, and Broadway still teaches the workshops. Many civic organizations have been established through the Leadership Classroom, including Black Nurses Rock and 100 Black Men of Syracuse. Broadway also was the principal consultant on the development of the City of Syracuse's neighborhood planning program, Tomorrow's Neighborhoods Today (TNT). TNT creates a comprehensive process for involving neighborhood residents, businesses and organizations in planning for their neighborhoods. It identifies and builds upon community assets, and develops workable plans and priorities. Nearly 20 years later, the TNT program is robust and inclusive, with an adopted slogan of Margaret Mead's, "Never doubt that a small group of thoughtful, committed citizens can change the world. Indeed, it is the only thing that ever has." Broadway's honors include the Syracuse University Falk College School of Social Work Social Justice Award (2017), Onondaga Community College John H. Mulroy Founder's Award (2017), and the New York State Senate Woman of Distinction (2012). Broadway holds a Master of Science degree in leadership and educational policy studies from Northern Illinois University and a Bachelor of Science degree in social work from Southern Illinois University. Her continuing education includes Marcellus Executive Leadership (2016) and Leadership Greater Syracuse (2004) programs. Early in her career, she served as director of field services for Literacy Volunteers of America in Syracuse.

Dr. Güner Arslan
Dialogue Institute Austin

1. How do you define social harmony?

To me, social harmony is achieved when all individuals and groups making up a society feel part of, contribute to, and enjoy the benefits of it. While this might be easier to do in a homogeneous society, it requires some serious effort in a truly diverse society. In this sense, I believe achieving social harmony should be the goal of every diverse community and deliberate effort need to be put in place to reach this goal.

We live in a time in the U.S. where the lack of harmony is becoming ever more evident. It seems like divisions across racial and ethnic lines, across political lines, across religious lines, and across socioeconomic lines are becoming ever deeper, especially with the amplifying effect of social media. Yet the work to build bridges across these divisions seems to be same as before: left to a few non-profits that genuinely try to bridge the gaps across these lines.

I believe social harmony is the fruit of loving and accepting each other as they are. It is a result of trying to see the world from the perspective of others and to understand how they feel. Only then can we treat the others in a way they like to be treated rather than what we think they should be treated like. "Hosgoru" is a Turkish word that is often translated into English as tolerance; however, this does not convey the real meaning. Tolerance to many people has a negative connotation. Hosgoru literary means to "to see beautifully" and implies an effort to see beautifully even if at first sight you cannot see the beauty. This is similar to the concept of "loving your neighbor." Love here is a commandment, not a feeling. You don't wait for the feeling to just come to you, rather you have to exhort some effort to reach a state where you feel the love.

Social harmony is a lofty goal but we are not going to get there unless we work for it. We at the Dialogue Institute Austin are committed to doing our share to reach this goal.

2. What is the best bridge-building technique you have come across or used?

The best technique by far is direct interaction between individuals and groups. This might not be the easiest or the most scalable solution, but it is, based on my experience, the most effective one. I can read about others in volumes of books, I can watch documentaries or movies, I can take courses and seminars and all these would help to understand others better, but none of these is the same as looking into the eyes of a person and listening to what they have to say.

Once a "we against them" mentality takes root in a person it is very hard to uproot it by using intellectual arguments. Information can be replaced by more accurate information but emotions cannot be replaced by any information. Emotions need to be replaced with other emotions. I don't know what magic goes on inside people's hearts and minds, but I can say from experience that breathing the same air and looking into the eyes of the other does change people generally for the better. This is why at the Dialogue Institute our motto is to "find excuses to bring people together."

3. What does your organization do to promote social harmony?

In the past sixteen plus years with The Dialogue Institute, we have tried numerous techniques to bring people together. We started with lecture series, seminars, conferences and such. We tried artistic events such as Interfaith Art Festivals and Whirling Dervishes performances. We tried interfaith and intercultural trips to various parts of the World where we not only visited must-see attractions but also made sure we visited locals in their homes and interacted with them. We also organized dinners and social gatherings. We have found that all of these different types of events do help with building bridges. You get really close with people when you travel with them for 10 days, you learn new perspectives when you sit in a lecture about another culture, the art and music of a different culture does help you get over some prejudices you might have but at the end my experience is that the best way to build bridges is to break bread together.

The famous 13th Century Muslim mystic Rumi said: "Come, come whoever you are..." and we started organizing events and asked people to come in a similar fashion. Over the years, however, we discovered that people are not very comfortable to go to new places where they are to meet new people and talk about new ideas. It is just too overwhelming to many. How were we then going to reach out to these people? We decided that instead of them coming to us, we should go to them and meet them in their places of worship where they feel safe. Furthermore, we decided to start the conversation with topics that they are familiar with or sometimes don't have any particular topics at all. One example is the fast-breaking dinner program that we organize in the Muslim holy month of Ramadan. We reach out to places of worship and tell them we would like to visit them and share our food with them. All we ask for is a place and time in their place worship where we can serve our food and that they show up to share the food with us.

Biography

Dr. Güner Arslan was born in Germany to Turkish parents, moved to Turkey with them and made it to Texas as soon as he could in 1998. He received his Ph.D. degree from the Electrical & Computer Engineering Department at the University of Texas at Austin in 2000.

While at graduate school he founded a student organization with his friends to start an interfaith dialogue on campus. The student organization grew into the Dialogue Institute, which is an education non-profit that is now active in six states with more than a dozen chapters. Güner leads the Dialogue Institute in Austin where he works with other volunteers on the mission of finding excuses to bring people together. He also speaks at different venues on Interfaith Dialogue and his faith tradition—Islam. Dr. Arslan is the chairman of the board of trustees of Houston based North American University and serves on the boards of Interfaith Action of Central Texas (iACT), Leadership Austin, and Raindrop Foundation Austin. He does all this on weekends and evenings as he is a full-time engineer at Silicon Laboratories developing algorithms for chips that power the Internet of Things (IoT).

Güner is a husband and a father of four children—a boy in High School and three girls in Middle School, Elementary School, and Pre-K. You can reach Güner at guner.arslan@dialogueatx.org.

Nora Bond
Convergence on Campus

1. How do you define social harmony?

The essence of social harmony is in the essence of musical harmony. Far from being ethereal and incomprehensible—though they may have that effect—musical harmonies are highly structured. Musical discord, and one could say social discord, is the opposite: abrupt, jarring, unsettling. The clues to social harmony, then, may be found in the structured nature of musical harmony, and one could even distill it to one statement: harmony depends on reference points. What makes discord unpleasant is its unpredictability and staccato, two characteristics that imply untrustworthiness and detachment. Humans are, rightfully, allergic to these traits.

Harmony, however, binds. Simultaneous sounds, produced in progressions, and with reference to one another, can create something bigger than one chord. Social harmony, then, is when people have a personal, positive reference point for all kinds of people. If one group isolates itself and declares its own eminence, it is like a single striking chord in the midst of a song—it is unwilling to reference everything around it. Instead, when a person encounters someone curious—perhaps with a different language, race, religion, or physical ability—and has a reference point to orient towards ("I've never seen anyone

186

like her before, but she's talking just like my fourth-grade teacher") harmony is more likely. Of course, the hard work of relationship building always follows initial interactions, but that first willingness, that first harkening back to something recognizable and positive is essential to moving through the first discomfort. So much potential social harmony is lost at that initial, split-second dismissal: I don't know anyone like you, I'm not going to engage.

Thus, very practically, social harmony is defined as the curiosity to seek new reference points—new understandings of people—and the structures that support this exploration. When institutions, policies, and communities are open, affirming, and oriented towards connection, it demonstrates an expectation for positive engagement.

At Convergence, we are particularly committed to ensuring that higher education is actively involved with forming positive reference points for religious, secular, and spiritual identities. Through policies and practices, institutions can support individuals in assimilating new conceptions of personhood. Social harmony depends on individuals and institutions conspiring to add more variety to our notions of how to be a human. Endeavoring towards the complexity is not easy or pleasant, but most worthy tasks, of course, aren't. Choosing to compose a symphony with variety is harder than bashing divergent notes, but the effort creates harmony.

2. What is the best bridge-building technique you have come across or used?

Metaphorical bridge-building is perhaps even more complicated than literal bridge-building. Although best practices often rightfully focus on dialogue, active listening, and repeatedly achieving mutual understanding, the most effective practice invisibly undergirds these. Self-awareness is the primary—as in both first and essential—technique needed. If one is in dialogue, attempting to fully listen, and willing to take on another's perspective, she must first be versed in what she brought with her, what she is likely to react to, and her own processes of meaning-making.

To borrow a phrase from the Center for Courage and Renewal's Circle of Trust® Touchstones, the process requires one to "Turn to wonder." Inevitably in bridge-building there are disagreements. Instead of immediately reacting, assuming one's superiority, or judging, the phrase calls us deeper into what, in ourselves, is responding. Our values, identities, and histories are ever-present, filtering our perceptions and ready to be summoned at first notice. If one is attempting to bridge-build with a person of a different faith but has a deeply rooted perception of the other faith as dangerous, there will be only negligible progress. If one is attempting to bridge-build with someone who reminds her of a childhood bully, there will also be only negligible progress. What a bridge-builder brings to the engagement is not inconsequential. Thus, when one feels that impulse—"I must be wary of anyone who practices this faith, I am inclined to not like you because you remind me of him" — she must recognize it and turn to wonder. What is it being provoked in me? How will I respond to myself, before I proceed? Am I in a place to host this conversation, knowing what it will bring up for me? How should I proceed, if my goal is really to co-create? Of all the best practices for bridge-building, self-awareness is the foundation. Only by welcoming and examining our impulses (which come from the least informed but most defensive parts of our brain) can we be open to bridge-building authentically and sustainably.

3. What does your organization do to promote social harmony?

Convergence On Campus is committed to enhancing campuses for religious, secular, and spiritual identities. In the same way that higher education is shifting to actively engage with different racial, ethnic, geographic, gender, socioeconomic status, and sexual identities (through physical centers on campus, stated policies, and trained staff) we aim to equip them to serve religious, secular, and spiritual identities.

Unfortunately, these identities are often omitted from diversity, equity, and inclusion work. Some dismiss our work claiming that public universities cannot legally engage these identities, or that religion is a private choice and expecting a university to support it is unreasonable. Convergence disagrees. Legally, of course, all students have a right to observance and accommodation. Institutionally, it is absurd to prefer to support some identities over others. Ethically, universities have chosen to hold themselves to the highest standards of student development, and choosing to engage with these identities is work that serves any student who walks on campus and simply desires to be him/her/their self. Creating campus communities who actively support all aspects of student identity is core to our vision.

Convergence's mission, though, pertains to bridge-building in another way. In our understanding of social harmony, people who have positive reference points for all sorts of people are more likely to engage and sustain relationships across difference. Making campuses supportive places for all religious, secular, and spiritual identities allows these identities to be explicit and sustained. A conservative Jewish woman is not penalized for not being in class on a High Holy Day. A secular student problematizes the school's Biblical motto at an event with the Dean. A student experiencing grief seeks a trained campus professional to explore his spiritual crisis. In each example, there are also the uncountable people whose daily life now include these expressions, people who now have positive references points for religious, secular, and spiritual identities.

Social harmony depends on normalizing the process of accepting new ideas. When the institution itself communicates that variety in religious, secular, and spiritual identities is expected and welcome, all students absorb this message. Most likely every student is not observing that Jewish holiday, but years later when a Jewish co-worker takes the same day off, that student isn't perturbed. A student who doesn't identify as secular will nonetheless see that the institution takes secular concerns seriously, and therefore it is worth understanding. Not every student will experience an existential crisis or name it that way, but knowing that there are people who are capable of helping when our perception of the world is shattered, can make a tremendous difference.

Convergence On Campus builds bridges in an active sense, by enhancing campus professionals' capacities to support religious, secular, and spiritual identities. But we also work to normalize the varieties of these identities to seed mutual respect in all students. By transforming higher education to allow for explicit expressions and institutional supports for these identities, we also change perceptions in students who aren't remotely interested in these identities—but who can now see them as legitimate, acceptable, and worthy. Sending students out into the world who are both affirmed in their various identities and free from illusions about religious, secular, and spiritual identities is our goal, and how we build bridges today.

Biography

Nora Bond is a higher education professional committed to improving campus capacity to support students, staff, and faculty as a whole, intersectional people. She is most passionate about building inclusive communities with faculty and staff on campuses. Most recently, she worked with the Office of Religious and Spiritual Life at Mount Holyoke College to create a student interfaith leadership council and a living-learning community. Previously, she worked with the Center for Courage & Renewal to evaluate a program designed to enhance relational trust within the adult communities of schools. Nora earned a B.A. in Psychology from Mount Holyoke College and an M.A. in Child Study and Human Development from Tufts University. She is a trained spiritual director and has worked in early education classrooms and professional development programs, as well as student resource departments in higher education.

Rev. Jon Mundy
All Faiths Seminary International

1. How do you define social harmony?

My go-to guide in all human relationship is *A Course in Miracles* and the Course is very clear that the way we treat others is the way we treat ourselves. To quote the Course:

If you attack error in another, you will hurt yourself. You cannot know your brother when you attack him. Attack is always made upon a stranger. You are making him a stranger by misperceiving him, and so you cannot know him. It is because you have made him a stranger that you are afraid of him. Perceive him correctly so that you can know him. There are no strangers in God's creation.

T-3.III.7:1-7

My main area of interest these days lies in exploring the Eastern Philosophy of dharma and its congruence with the teaching of the Course. Dharma signifies *the cosmic law and order that make life and the universe possible*. It denotes the *purification* and *moral transformation* of human beings. For Sikhs, it means the path of righteousness and proper spiritual practices.

A central concept in the Rig Veda (perhaps the world's oldest scripture) is that created beings fulfill their true nature when they follow the path set for them by *the ordinance of the universe*.

Failing to follow these principles is not a sin. It simply means that failing to follow these principles leads to miscreation which then inevitably leads to purification and then back to success when the selfish mind fails in its own efforts and must then realign with the Mind of God.

Very simply put, as Jesus says it in the Gospels, "Do unto others as you would have others do unto you." Everything we do, every thought, every word, and every deed has its effect in the universe. The more I can control my own thoughts, my own words and my own deeds the closer I come to bringing my own mind in alignment with the Divine Mind. The more I come to love my brothers and sisters who "are" me, i.e., there is not a difference between us—except in time.

Time is the schoolhouse in which we learn of our oneness and knowing only Oneness we must treat others as we would treat ourselves.

2. What is the best bridge-building technique you have come across or used?

Obviously, the best bridge-building technique comes in the acceptance of responsibility for my own thoughts and actions, which comes in the deep realization of the most fundamental law there is in the Universe, again to quote the Course:

If I intervened between your thoughts and their results, I would be tampering with a basic law of cause and effect; the most fundamental law there is. I would hardly help you if I depreciated the power of your own thinking. This would be in direct opposition to the purpose of this course. It is much more helpful to remind you that you do not guard your thoughts carefully enough. You may feel that at this point it would take a miracle to enable you to do this, which is perfectly true. You are not used to miracle-minded thinking, but you can be trained to think that way. All miracle workers need that kind of training.

T-2.VII.1:4-10

Again, everything is up to me. It's how I choose to see my brother that matters. I love the definition of Jesus from the Course.

Jesus was a man but saw the face of Christ in all his brothers and remembered God.

C-5.II.1

i.e., Jesus saw the false without accepting it as true.

3. What does your organization do to promote social harmony?

All Faiths Seminary International seeks to provide and much education for our student as we can with an emphasis on the congruence i.e., the sameness within everyone, of every cultural and religious tradition.

Biography

Rev. Jon Mundy, Ph.D. is an author, lecturer, the publisher of Miracles magazine and the Executive Director of All Faiths Seminary International in New York City. The author of 11 books, his newest book is *A Course in Mysticism and Miracles*. His earlier book, *Living A Course in Miracles* now exists in 8 different languages.

Dr. Mehnaz M. Afridi
The Holocaust, Genocide and Interfaith Education Center at Manhattan College

1. How do you define social harmony?

Society seems to have been the cornerstone of any civilization to keep communities, families, and individuals together. Some thinkers have said that we need one another to function as a society and we have to build harmony to survive both economically and emotionally. Societal norms have transformed over time according to the needs of a society especially when human beings have felt oppressed, exploited or victimized. In the

United States, the oppression of African Americans is an example how society has changed its rules and laws but we still have remnants of racism and oppression that glare at us from within society every day. I believe that memory plays a deep role in these issues, memory of how "things were" "should be" and "are." For example, the memories that communities have about one another and the reconstruction of these through oral and written history tell the next story of social harmony. If we could offer the future generations positive and explicate the traumatic memories of our generations then perhaps we can have what I would call social harmony. Responsibility, truth, and self-criticism of each community can culminate in a diverse and harmonious society.

2. What is the best bridge-building technique you have come across or used?

I use various tools to build bridges and one the most effective one is how you tell a story when there are conflicting narratives in a room. I work with many Catholics, Muslims, and Jews to build bridges and have been able to deal with very challenging topics by following some hard but simple rules:

1. Listen to the narrative of the other
2. Emotional responses are not effective
3. Acknowledge the pain of the other
4. Be self-critical
5. Be truthful about the scars of your community in the past

For example, I take from the following lessons: In 2016, I visited Berlin, Germany where I was invited for the release of the third German edition of responses to *Die Sonnenblume* by Simon Wiesenthal as I was invited to write a response from a Muslim perspective. I met many Germans who were interested in my role as a Muslim woman teaching Islam and also directing a Holocaust Center. Their questions came from shock and dismay perhaps a backlash, I wondered as they inquired how I could possibly be entrapped in two polarizing and extreme visions of the world: Jewish & Muslim. The most startling comments were how I could call myself a Muslim since I did not wear the hijab and why I would be deeply committed to Holocaust education, and lastly, could I not find something better to do! Some comments horrified my American and now Berliner host such as; "Voting for Hitler was the only thing we could have done!" Awkward silence and brisk acknowledgments by the local Berliners became a stark message to me that somehow my identity was sterilized and my work on the Holocaust had been battered in the most apologetic country of European crimes during World War II. I continued to speak with the local Germans and ask questions that they had never confronted, not about the Holocaust but their own feelings of loss as they experienced a million Syrians migrate into what they assumed was only a German country. These locals became engaged in these issues by building an understanding between them and myself.

Recently, I was invited to Miami, Florida to speak for the local Muslim community on Jewish-

Muslim relations, then I was invited to speak to a few leaders. I sat with five respectful and professional Muslim men who are considered leaders in the Muslim-American communities in Miami, a city with a large Jewish population. I was there to have a conversation about Muslim perceptions of Jews and how we can change our view taking into consideration the principles of Islam. I was asked the following questions about Jews: "Don't you think they control political events? Aren't they all rich?" Some of them had never asked those questions openly and I was there as a Muslim to respond. This intimate conversation is one of several I have had about the perception of Jews in Muslim communities, whether they are Turkish, Indian, Pakistani, Saudi, Iraqi, or others. We discussed the Shoah, and I was instantly confronted with questions about other genocides in comparison. This discussion was immensely important in many ways: first, it allowed male Muslim leaders to listen to a Muslim woman speak about Jews; second, it offered a reference point in the religion when they go out in the community; and finally, they were open to pursuing the deepening of Jewish–Muslim relations. One of the many issues that were brought up was the concern about the Qur'anic scriptures that discuss Jews or Christians in a negative light. The Qur'an has many such verses that can be negative and ambiguous for the non-Muslim and especially Muslims. And, on the other hand, my work with Jewish community leaders is led by the following question at times: "Is the Qur'an anti-Semitic?" My response is clearly: no. Such a response requires that we understand the

Qur'an and the representations of Jews in the Islamic tradition. Teaching at a Lasallian Catholic College as a Muslim woman both Islam and the Holocaust has been an amazing opportunity and I can confidently say that my work at the Center and the dept. of Religious Studies is in itself a living testimony of interfaith work.

These incidences and many more have strengthened my work on the Shoah and my Islamic identity and both Muslims and Jews compelled me to think about memory. The challenges I face are Holocaust denial, relativization or blatant anti-Semitism seeped in the words: Israel and Zionism. The challenges I face personally as a Muslim is the Islamophobia on the streets, the perceptions of Muslims, women and immigrant policies that have isolated many. Most of these challenges have been wrought with how we through generations in these specific communities think of one another or as I say "remember each other" or even "acknowledge" one another's history? My work on the Holocaust, Shoah is about bringing the stories of millions alive because I believe that as people of different identities and communities, we need to speak up for one another. How I ask, can we build bridges in this climate?

How has one learned to recall the "other's" tradition? What moments in history are the ones that define us and those that do not? David Rieff's book *In Praise of Forgetting: Historical Memory and its Ironies*, he asks the important questions of memory, tradition, and ethics. He further questions how and what we choose to commemorate, forgive and forget. What shall I

Never forget; the loss, the death and the need for humans to kill and destroy my identity? David Rieff's chapter entitled, "Must we deform the past in order to preserve it," resonated with me in two ways; one that memory of a particular past is framed morally by human beings as either positive or negative in this case a deformed memory as Rieff puts it, two that Nostalgia (or how one recollects the past) can protect or destroy memory as he further states: "At some point in time, will not Nazi atrocities, collaboration, even the Shoah itself become …plain history?" My question is how do we transition our own memories that are not only the creation of our community's memory but how do we deform the memories of the other to protect our own narrative? I wondered many times, whether I ever did crawl out of my zone and confront the memory of someone else's' past? And does this move have a morality in order for us to move beyond the memory of an old enemy, perpetrator, and murderer? This was what compelled some of the work I did in my book but more importantly, I wanted to ask some deeper questions about the construction of who we are against someone else's sensation of memory.

3. What does your organization do to promote social harmony?

My organization, The Holocaust, Genocide and Interfaith Education Center at Manhattan College has many programs and peacebuilding events in the community.

1. Social service to the elderly especially survivors
2. Teaming up Jews, Catholics and Muslims for projects
3. Building programs around anti-Semitism and Islamophobia
4. Reaching out to minorities and programs in the Bronx

My college's mission is also directed at bringing social harmony by the Lasallian Mission, which states:

- Faith in the Presence of God. The Lasallian School nurtures belief in the living presence of God in our world
- Concern for the Poor and Social Justice
- Respect for All Persons
- Inclusive Community

This mission is also aligned with our own Center focusing on eradicating human suffering and learning from the lessons of the Holocaust.

Biography

Dr. Afridi is an Associate Professor of Religious studies and Director of Holocaust, Genocide, and Interfaith Education Center at Manhattan College. She teaches Islam, Holocaust, Genocide, and issues of gender within Islam. Her articles have appeared in books such as; *Sacred Tropes: Tanakh, New Testament, and Qur'an as Literature and Culture*, (Brill, 2006). *Not Your Father's*

Anti-Semitism: Hatred of the Jews in the 21st Century (Paragon House, 2008). 2018. *"A Muslim's Response to Frank H. Littel"* in *Legacy of an Impassioned Plea Franklin H. Littel's Crucifixion of the Jews*, Ed. David Patterson, (New York: Paragon Press), 2018. *"Muslim Memory and Righting Relations with the Other"* in *Righting Relations After the Holocaust*, Eds. Elena G. Procario-Foley and Robert A. Cathey, (New Jersey: Paulist Press). *"The Role of Muslims and the Holocaust"* in Oxford Handbooks Online, (Oxford University Press, 2015). She is the co-editor of a book entitled: *"Orhan Pamuk and Global Literature: Existentialism and Politics"* (May 2012, Palgrave Macmillan), and her recent book *Shoah through Muslim Eyes* (Academic Studies Press, 2017) has been nominated for the Yad Vashem International Book Prize for Holocaust Research and the Jacob Schnitzer Book Award. Dr. Afridi obtained her Ph.D. from the University of South Africa, her MA and BA from Syracuse University.

Rev. Scott Quinn
Marin Interfaith Council

1. How do you define social harmony?

Social harmony is the ability and willingness to listen to, connect with, and even potentially be changed by interacting with others, particularly those who come from different backgrounds. If we use a musical analogy, how might each distinct "melody" be heard in its uniqueness and affirmed so that the collection of melodies forms a harmony? The music does not become homogeneous, but rather distinct differences are valued, explored and encouraged to be expressed.

In social harmony, there is a particular concern for those whose views and wellbeing have been discounted. Their experiences and perspectives have often been overlooked, the result being that a veneer of harmony might exist, but it fails to include those whose stories are not part of the culturally dominant narrative. Social harmony seeks to foster the beloved community referenced by Dr. Martin Luther King, Jr. and others, by promoting a society in which everyone thrives and is welcome.

2. What is the best bridge-building technique you have come across or used?

The best bridge-building technique is active listening with an open heart and mind. When we meet someone who is "different" or "other," can we suspend our pre-conceived notions long enough to see a whole human being rather than a label or belief system? For instance, if you are a cisgender Christian and have a deep conversation with a person who is Muslim or Transgender, you are not meeting with Islam or the entire Transgender community, you are meeting with a full human being for whom their religion or gender-identity is a key part of their human experience, but it neither defines nor determines their entire personhood. We meet individuals not religious or ethnicities or sexual orientations or any other label/group. When doing active listening, we also listen not just for a person's beliefs and views, but we are also curious about experiences that form those perspectives. We say, "That's a fascinating perspective that is different than mine. Would you be willing to share with me an experience you've had that shapes your view?" We are always encountering a unique human being, whose experiences, gifts, and paradoxes exceed any single affiliation or label.

3. What does your organization do to promote social harmony?

We have convened difficult conversations in which a safe space is created for those with differing views to hear one another and build bridges of understanding. While a consensus may not always be reached, we seek to create an environment where loving curiosity can flourish; a space in which both similarities and differences can be honored. As one faith leader is fond of saying, "We may not all be like-minded, but we can be like-hearted."

One example is our "Love Lives in Marin" initiative, which seeks to promote a radical welcome for all persons in our community: all races, religions, gender identities, sexual orientations, countries of origin, ethnicities, and abilities. We have held vigils, rallies, online/social media sharing, and panel discussions that provide venues for a wide variety of individuals to share their stories. By highlighting stories of inclusion and social harmony, we hope to generate more of the same. As people see social harmony in action, they are inspired to create more of it; they realize ways in which they are already living and witnessing the beloved community.

Most especially, this initiative welcomes persons from marginalized communities to share their experiences of living within the dominant culture, as well as offering their messages of hope, inspiration, resilience, and challenge to those who welcome the opportunity to listen, learn and be in solidarity with them.

Learn more at:
www.LoveLivesInMarin.org

Biography

Scott Quinn is Executive Director of the Marin Interfaith Council. He was ordained a Lutheran minister and was an educator and spiritual director at an interfaith spirituality center in Austin that was part of a Catholic healthcare system. He is Core Faculty for the Spiritual Direction Program at The Chaplaincy Institute, an interfaith seminary/community in Berkeley. Scott lives in San Rafael where he has a spiritual direction/supervision practice.

www.scottquinn.net.

Rev. Rhonda Schienle
World AWAKE

1. How do you define social harmony?

I define social harmony as meeting all people or groups of people right where they are without judgment.

One of our United States Supreme Court Justices, Ruth Bader Ginsburg once said: "The true symbol of America is not the bald eagle, it is the pendulum; when the pendulum swings too far one way, it will come back." This is to say that the pendulum comes back to balance or in the social environment, harmony.

2. What is the best bridge-building technique you have come across or used?

To listen often with care and compassion for and with others is one of the best bridge-building techniques I have utilized. Listening and acknowledging another human being is a wonderful gift to give and fosters bridge-building. Also, when one remembers what another believes, does not take away or remove anything from who you are.

3. What does your organization do to promote social harmony?

Our organization, World AWAKE, is reaching out to the community, listening, meeting them where they are and offering peace.

Biography

Rev. Rhonda L. Schienle became an Ordained Interfaith Minister in 2011 through the American Institute of Holistic Theology and Order of Universal Interfaith. In the spring of 2017, Rev. Rhonda was proud to become her own publisher and wrote her first book entitled *"Sister Sage's*

Astrological Journeys." Rev. Rhonda Schienle founded Interfaith Ministry Services LLC of Northwest Indiana region. She enjoys working within the full circle of life experiences. This includes weddings, spiritual baptism, celebrations of life and facilitating spiritual classes. Currently, she is proudly serving as Board Chair for World AWAKE, an InterSpiritual, InterFaith, InterConnected Community Linking Spirit and Service. Rev. Rhonda survived stage 3-breast cancer and a near-death experience in 2007. She is a business owner, speaker, teacher, writer, and entrepreneur.

Clay Boykin
Men's Fellowship Network

1. How do you define social harmony?

The richness in colors and textures found in a tapestry is a display of social harmony. No two threads, colors, or parts of the tapestry are identical, yet this is where the beauty is found. Compassion and respect for one another's culture and circumstance are the foundation; the warp and weft of the tapestry and the warp and weft of social harmony.

2. What is the best bridge-building technique you have come across or used?

My father traveled and lived around the world as an agriculture economist. His role was to help increase crop and livestock yields. Rather than going in with a preconceived idea of who the people were and what needed to be done, Dad took time beforehand to study the history of the culture and region seeking to understand the background as to why farming and ranching was being done the way it was. This provided a frame of reference that enabled him to engage meaningfully with his clients whether they were in Africa, Syria, Pakistan or Iran. He would tell me, first seek to understand and then be understood.

3. What does your organization do to promote social harmony?

The Men's Fellowship Network is a community that supports men in connecting and growing along our spiritual journeys. We are an inclusive group where all men are welcome to gather in a safe non-judgmental environment and move from our heads and speak our truth with an open heart. Our overarching topic is "male spirituality" and we come at it from many different directions, such as: Fear, Vulnerability, Dark Night of the Soul, Compassion, Forgiveness, Deep Listening, and more.

Biography

Clay Boykin is a former United States Marine Corps artillery officer from a small Texas town who climbed the corporate ladder and one day found himself working on Park Avenue. His life took a radical turn at age 53 while on vacation when chest pains led to a mystical experience and emergency quintuple bypass surgery. Other life challenges ensued and several years later Clay emerged from his dark night of the soul a spirit-centered man. Using his 38 years of business experience and a deeply entrenched servant leadership approach, Clay founded the Men's Fellowship Network in 2012. He has facilitated hundreds of weekly circles and made long lasting friendships through the network, which has invested over 20,000 man-hours in the overarching theme of male spirituality.

Clay published his first book, *Circles of Men*, in 2018, which quickly made it into the Amazon top 100 list in the category of Self Help/Spirituality. Circles of Men examines the lessons he and his fellow male seekers have learned from gathering in their trusting and supportive network and weekly circle.

Rev. Laura M. George
The Oracle Institute

1. How do you define social harmony?

As a student of history and founder of a spiritual think tank called The Oracle Institute (*www.TheOracleInstitute.org*), I take a very long and broad view of humanity's evolution toward social harmony. I take into account the various ages of mankind (i.e., Industrial Age, Information Age, etc.), the birth and extension of the world's religions (e.g.: the Axial Age and the current spread of pluralism), the health and expansion of democracy across the globe (e.g.: the U.S. failure to spread democracy in the Middle East), and the acceptance and adoption of human rights (e.g.: LGBTQ rights). There simply is no other logical perspective from which to approach the topic of social harmony, other than viewing it as an agonizingly slow, epochal, yet steady march toward harmony. Indeed, to approach this topic otherwise would cause paralyzing sadness and make me too depressed to opine on the subject at all!

Thus, Oracle's approach to observing and defining social change is via Integral Theory, conceived by Ken Wilber—the "Einstein of Consciousness" and the only philosopher to be taught in his own lifetime. For those unfamiliar with Wilber's work, think of it as Abraham Maslow on steroids and a grand extension of the Spectrum of Consciousness, originally mapped in the 1960s by another of my heroes, Dr. Clare Graves. These models afford us the lens through which to track social harmony and predict its gradual dissemination around the world.

After laying the above foundation for my competency to address the question and for brevity's sake, I will simply define "social harmony" as both a person's and his/her community's consistent exercise of the Golden Rule—stated in nearly duplicative form by every major religion and wisdom tradition. Clearly, "doing unto others as you would have done to yourself and to your community" is the hallmark of any group of humans who are ready, willing, and able to practice social harmony. As I have defined it, social harmony likely is practiced by a majority of humans but by a minority of nation-states, which sadly means it is not yet practiced reliably on a global level.

2. What is the best bridge-building technique you have come across or used?

What Maslow's Hierarchy of Needs, the Spectrum of Consciousness, and Integral Theory plainly reveal is that human evolution is not moving as quickly as we would want, nor as quickly as the challenges of the 21st Century demand. In the Post-Modern Age, we are witnessing a clash of cultures the world has never seen. Why? Because the Spectrum of Consciousness is so varied that there are barbarians (i.e., people with impulsive, low-level needs and drives) walking the earth alongside avatars (i.e., people who have reached or are closing in on the advanced state of enlightenment). While this may sound hyperbolic, it is the truth. Incidentally, objective truth does exist, despite the current trend toward dismantling and debasing it.

To clarify my point, let me briefly summarize some of the conclusions we have reached at The Oracle Institute, thanks to our careful study of Integral Theory: When humans existed thousands of years ago, everyone operated at just a few levels of existence. You were either in the aristocratic and privileged class and you exploited your power, you were a merchant or a warrior and you enjoyed a modicum of control over your life experience, or you were a serf who had nothing more to hope for than ample food, shelter, and sex.

But today, we see many classes or levels of the human experience. There still are people struggling for their very existence, but at the other end of the spectrum are those who have not only managed to overcome all base level needs—including materialism—they have begun to self-actualize and reach states of non-duality! Such humans did not exist in the past, except as leaders of religious movements (e.g.: Jesus, Buddha). So to even speak of "social harmony" means that there now are enough humans on the planet who hold this value as a treasured goal.

To bridge the ever-widening gap between the spiritual "haves" and the material "have-nots" (which is an extreme oversimplification of the spectrum) requires a great deal of expertise. At Oracle, we call this divide the "God Gap," and we rack our brains and search our hearts every day to figure out how to bridge the great chasm created by the resultant culture wars. Would that there existed a magic key—just one key that could unlock the evolutionary impulse in everyone!

The reality is that there is no one magic key. Instead, there are numerous approaches to spreading social harmony and those methods differ depending toward whom you wish to apply the balm of love. For every meme loves. The issue is to what extent humans are capable of extending their love, whether it be a tribal extension, an ethnocentric sharing, or a global comprehension of interconnectedness that leads to the purest form of social harmony.

Consequently, those of us who wish to spread altruistic morals need to have a firm grasp of how humans *"transcend and include"* their worldviews. Everyone has the capacity for growth, and collectively we slowly are reaching greater levels of social harmony. Yet individually we contribute to the expansion of altruism and enlightened values—such as social harmony—only after we experience the satiation of lower level needs (e.g., transcending poverty). Even then, only some of us will reach the higher states of consciousness, which allow us to feel empathy toward our fellow man, interfaith acceptance, and social egalitarianism.

To summarize, spreading social harmony is possible only when an individual and his culture are properly evaluated and then realistically addressed. Like a doctor making a diagnosis and giving a prescription, peacebuilders need the skillset to evaluate a person's capacity to live harmoniously and then suggest the correct approach to raise spiritual standards. There is no quick fix, just the potential for achieving incremental, lasting, positive change.

3. What does your organization do to promote social harmony?

At Oracle, we have implemented a number of programs that we believe add to a climate of harmony and a culture of peace. After the tragic events of September 11, 2001, we began as an interfaith charity in the affluent northern Virginia region. Our programming included multi-faith classes and publishing books aimed at both the post-religious (i.e., New Age) and Christian audience. We were successful in reaching the pluralistic suburbanites in that affluent area, but we also felt their spiritual needs were being met by numerous organization in and around the Nation's' Capitol. So in 2010, we decided to move to the tip of the Bible Belt to actively engage the people in the Appalachian Mountains of southwestern Virginia—a culture that is notoriously suspect of pluralistic and progressive values. Immediately, we met with opposition when we sought to build our headquarters—the Peace Pentagon—and we were nearly run out of town by a series of legal challenges (good thing I was an attorney!). Since then, we have softened our approach and adjusted our methods for interacting with the predominantly Evangelical population of this region. We also became Ken Wilber enthusiasts when we learned about Integral Theory and its capacity to assist us in helping others achieve horizontal and vertical growth.

Some more definitions will be helpful in explaining our work: Horizontal growth starts by identifying where someone lies on the Spectrum of Consciousness, feeling their push-back to educational materials that represent too much change, and rather than trying to move them up the spectrum to a totally new level of compassion, we instead help them expand their love within their comfort zone. Whereas vertical growth can occur with low hanging fruit (i.e., someone who truly is ready to transcend their old worldview), by helping them move up the spectrum to the next level of spiritual comprehension and loving expression.

For those who are ready for more advanced expressions of social harmony, we offer affirmative peacebuilding classes. For instance, in 2015 Oracle co-sponsored the Building the New World Conference, which was targeted at New

Age and "Second-Tier" humans. One more definition: Second Tier refers to people who have fully integrated a world-centric mindset and who are compelled to assist humanity. In 2016, we launched the Peace Pentagon HUB (*www.PeacePentagon.net*), an online platform for Sacred Activism. Last year, we started classes on the "Future of the Peace Movement." We focused on The Earth Constitution, which has been proposed by academics leading the Earth Federation Movement. Currently, we are co-sponsoring a Peace Congress in Washington, D.C., an effort of more than 200 peace groups.

Lastly, I would be remiss if I failed to include one more thought on how to achieve social harmony. I deeply believe that there can be no harmony until we collectively acknowledge and work to remediate global climate change. Oracle is a charitable partner in The Aluna Fund (*www.ICVgroup.org/the-aluna-fund*), which is dedicated to the "Unification of People and Planet." I am excited to be working with indigenous peoples on this project, and I am happy to report that sharing the "Original Instructions" for planet Earth tends to resonate with people across most of the Spectrum of Consciousness.

In closing, we at The Oracle Institute never miss an opportunity to brainstorm and experiment on how best to promote social harmony. We truly are grateful for the opportunity to be part of this new book by Harmony Interfaith Initiative, and we extend our heartfelt optimism for the future of humanity.

Biography

Rev. Laura M. George, J.D. is the Executive Director of The Oracle Institute, an educational charity that serves as an Advocate for Peace and a Vanguard for Conscious Evolution. Oracle is a spiritual think-tank headquartered at the Peace Pentagon in Independence, VA. Oracle operates an award-winning publishing house, multi-faith spirituality school, interfaith church, and peacebuilding practice. Laura also oversees the Peace Pentagon HUB, a strategic center, and networking site, and she helps manage the Valley of Light micro-community, with the goal of promoting a Culture of Peace through Spiritual Growth and Sacred Activism. Laura authored Oracle's award-winning foundational trilogy: The Truth: About the Five Primary Religions; The Love: Of the Fifth Spiritual Paradigm; and The Light: And the New Human (due 2019).

Steve Harper
The Ripple Effect

1. How do you define social harmony?

I define social harmony as a relationship between people who can overcome their experiential biases, situational blindness and leverage the power of real presence to be fully engaged with other human beings.

In today's distracted, soundbite culture, too many of us operate from a level of surface connection where we barely engage with other people and allow snap judgments and self-serving intentions to steer. This disingenuous approach leads us to create a culture of inharmonious interactions and social instability.

I believe that social harmony can only exist when all parties involved overcome the default autopilot behavior, which appears to be more of the norm and come to the table fully committed to engage, communicate and learn from others.

2. What is the best bridge-building technique you have come across or used?

In my work and research, I have found that every human being has some very basic but important requirements that have to be met before he or she can be fully engaged with other people. All humans have an innate need to feel seen, heard and understood on the most basic level. When these initial conditions are met then people allow themselves to feel or to be seen as useful, important, appreciated and even loved.

Though it seems like it might take a long time to help make conditions perfect for someone to feel all of that, it really doesn't. It just takes a mindful approach to an engagement with someone to accelerate the connection and relationship building process.

The best technique to build the essential bridge of connection is to be inquisitive about them. Asking what I call origin-focused questions can give tremendous insight into their background and backstory. One of my favorite questions is "Where are you from originally?" Everyone comes from somewhere and there's often a really enlightening story about how they got from where they were to where they are right now. It's a softball question that people unconsciously appreciate because it allows them to answer with the context and content they are absolutely experts in—their life. I find that this simple question immediately relaxes people and if you're prepared to spur the conversation on with some inquisitive follow-up questions, your rapport grows stronger. Their story provides you with a pretty incredible and insightful look into who this person is at their core.

3. What does your organization do to promote social harmony?

Through my company The Ripple Effect, my truest passion is helping people understand the importance of connection. Whether it's working with a company or an individual, we focus on helping identify, develop and grow the key relationships they depend on for their success.

In our work, connection is the "binding element" that drives every opportunity, every client relationship, employee retainage, the organizational leadership approach and of course organization's social presence within the community. Social harmony seems like an altruistic goal but when you truly look at it, it is the absolute zenith of our existence. It is essential in helping us coexist. Social harmony helps us get along in our work, our daily interactions and most importantly through our connection and the relationships we have with one another.

We promote social harmony by asking every

one of us to show up each and every day prepared to put forth the best versions of ourselves and be open to others. Does it always happen? No. But we try.

Biography

Steve Harper has become one of the most sought-after speakers and business strategists on the power of deepening and strengthening the power of connections through a process he calls "Rippling." Steve's unique and refreshing approach to how and why individuals, organizations and even our society can and must reach outside the box to connect, is literally changing lives. A serial entrepreneur, professional speaker, author and leading business strategist, Steve has successfully uncovered the secret to creating powerful long-lasting connections and their impact on one's personal and professional life. Steve has transitioned his years of business experience and unyielding customer focus into a successful consulting practice appropriately named *The Ripple Effect* after his successful first book by the same title. Steve has always maintained a unique focus on developing strong, long-lasting relationships with his clients, prospects, and employees. By building a strong network of referrals and repeat customers, Steve has honed his ability to foster client relationships into a leveraged system for achieving solid business success. That system is represented in his book *The Ripple Effect* and through his speaking engagements and customized speaking and workshop programs.

Dr. Elizabeth Debold
One World in Dialogue

1. How do you define social harmony?

Social harmony has not been a term that I have used in my work, although it is a very generative one. Immediately, one gets a sense of difference and unity—in harmony, the various tones from our voices or instruments come together in a fuller, vibrant, resonant whole. A culture that has social harmony would be one where differences are held together through a shared resonance that includes discord. Let me unpack that a bit.

Harmony, without discord, easily becomes kitsch—inauthentically sweet. Kitsch, in sociopolitical terms, would be expressed in an idealized traditionalism that suppresses dissent or difference. While harmonics implies voices coming together, if harmonizing only expresses an ongoing repetition within an evenly spaced range of notes, it becomes stultifying. I think of some of my favorite Gregorian chants: at the abbey dedicated to Hildegard von Bingen where the nuns sing at the very top of the register, their voices quavering together like angels' wings. This music is otherworldly, intentionally so. Its pure harmonies send thrills up the spine, opening up to heavenly realms. But we don't live there. There is no room for the range of our humanity and our well-earned differences in these gorgeous chants.

So, social harmony has to include dissonance. How can harmony and dissonance create a whole?

This is really our current predicament. Western culture has no shared harmonic, no shared song that we are all singing. The values that once held the West together have lost their power. We no longer are singing in the same key. It's not merely tunelessness or a tin ear, but a deeper sense of not sharing something ineffable that gives different subcultural groups a shared sense of humanity, purpose, and direction. There is too much discord and not enough harmony.

There isn't a simple way forward. No conductor of the cultural "orchestra" is going to set the key and beat and bring us together. In fact, the desire for one person—one man—to take over the baton and force us to sing together is dangerous. The idea of social harmony is so useful precisely because harmony is only creating by coming together in a multiplicity of voices, even when there is discord.

But, again, what can hold us together when we no longer are singing in the same key and the discord blares over the tune? Here we need to go deeper. Where does all sound come out of? Silence. When we no longer focus on one particular tune or set of beliefs, can we recognize that every voice emerges from silence?

Silence is recognition that at the heart of all of life, every part of society, is a mystery. As human beings, we each share this mystery of life and are forced—sooner or later—to confront the fact that we cannot control or know it. Here lies the potential for social harmony: if we can open up and acknowledge the roaring silence that unites us and exists prior to any voice or song, then we can honor the whole in its harmony and discord.

Social harmony can only be achieved if we are willing to see to the depth of what unites us — the silence — rather than getting caught on the different tunes and keys that we are singing in.

2. What is the best bridge-building technique that you have come across or used?

I don't know that bridge-building can ever actually be a "technique." The word "technique" implies something instrumental. "I" over here, act on "you" over there, for a specific purpose through which you become an instrument to achieve my goal, aim, or desire. To build a bridge to another person with views or opinions that are very different from my own, I cannot approach through the comfortable distance of applying a technique. To build a bridge, I must be the bridge — through my attentive listening, interest, and not knowing. I start from knowing that we share a common humanity, no matter what. We become who we are, with the beliefs that we have, through very understandable reactions and responses to the opportunities and difficulties in our lives.

Listening, interest, and not knowing are not a technique. They cannot be faked or manufactured for the moment. In a highly charged situation, such pretense will be seen through very quickly. Listening means to listen with the aim of understanding what another is saying without an agenda of one's own. How can we understand another human being in their terms, not ours? To do so, one listens not from the analytical, judging mind, but from the whole of our experience. Mind, body, and heart attuned to the other human being, seeking resonance and wondering at what seems dissonant. For this, one brings interest — a genuine curiosity that is not seeking for itself. Being truly interested is an act of compassion. And to keep our interest alive and open, we need to come from an inner position of not already knowing. We don't pre-judge or nod along with what someone is saying, because we want to take their words in fresh, new, and encounter them, coming from this unique person, on their own. It calls us to ask genuine questions, not to interrogate another or to assume that we understand. And it calls us to be sensitive to the space between us, the field of intimacy that arises through such deep attention to another human being. Such intimacy can be intimidating or too much, which we need to be aware of also, so that we allow another human to have the space and dignity to be themselves.

3. What does your organization do to promote social harmony?

Through the programs of One World in Dialogue, we aim to create a field of connectedness that spans the globe. We are not working in particular conflict zones or across stark lines of difference and antagonism, but are bringing together people who live in different cultures and who are interested in meeting at a deep level. We are trying to develop a sense of shared humanity as a reference point for living together on this planet. A "reference point" is a before-thought sense of being connected in a shared humanity before the arising of difference. From this point of unity, we engage in our differences. It provides a very different starting point for dialogue.

We see our work as a form of "subtle activism." Subtle activism works at a different level than traditional activism. We seek, in a sense, to change the frequency or resonance between us rather than striving to change policies or attitudes. While direct action in the social and political arena is necessary to hold governments and corporations accountable and to create social structures, subtle activism seeks to change the field between us that grounds our attitudes and explicit actions.

This can be tricky to understand. The subtle field between us guides how we respond and what we are capable of thinking. In an individualistic culture in which we assume that we are agents of our own destiny, this is hard to make sense of. But if you think about the difference between attending a religious service for the death of a dearly loved one and a New Year's Eve bash, perhaps it becomes clear. In the presence of the grief of loss, and one's encountering mortality, we tend to slow down and feel the poignancy of the human predicament. It would feel horrible if someone screamed, "Woohoo! Let's boogie!!" at the side of the grave of the departed. The context and atmosphere created by our loss and reflection creates a sense of what is appropriate and we tend to respond accordingly. The subtle dimension—the atmosphere between us—shapes our thoughts and actions.

So, imagine if, no matter who one encountered, we felt/sensed that we are human before we noticed, ah, this is a man or woman, here is a Black or White person, or is this a Muslim or Christian? It is a very different starting point to whatever comes next: passing in the street, a transaction in a shop, or the beginning of a deep dialogue. Our work is to cultivate that deeper sense of our common humanity through an awakening to the shared space between us and to learn how to dialogue from this starting point.

In sum, we pay attention to a dimension of precious sacredness that comes alive between us when we truly listen and see each other. This sacredness arises from the mystery of Life that we all are confronted with and deepens when we become aware that this is what we share most deeply. Dialogue from this point opens a new potential of difference-in-unity that is itself a new form of social harmony.

Biography

Elizabeth Debold, Ed.D., is a leading authority on gender development and author of the New York Times Notable Book of the Year *Mother Daughter Revolution* (Addison-Wesley, 1993; Bantam, 1994).

For the past three decades, she has worked on the front lines of gender and cultural evolution as activist, researcher, journalist, consciousness explorer, and transformative educator.

As a founding member of the Harvard Project on Women's Psychology and Girls' Development, directed by Dr. Carol Gilligan, she made critical theoretical contributions to understanding the cultural roots of gender difference. Widely acknowledged for the power of these insights into women's and men's development, she has developed acclaimed programming based on her research for organizations such as the Ms. Foundation for Women, the Shift Network, Miss Hall's School, and others. Currently on the faculty of Meridian University's Leadership & Social Transformation Program, she served as Academic Director of The Graduate Institute's Master of Arts program in Conscious Evolution and has also taught at Harvard University and the New School for Social Research. Dr. Debold has been sought as an expert on gender and the evolution of culture by major media outlets in the U.S. and abroad and has lectured in the U.S., Canada, Australia, and Europe. Her work has appeared in academic publications, popular media, international anthologies and now in the German-language magazine, evolve, where she is part of the editorial team and writes a regular feature on gender. Dr. Debold is a Senior Fellow of the Institute for Cultural Evolution (www.culturalevolution.org), and the founder of One World in Dialogue (www.oneworldindialogue.com), a global conversation space for people keen on transforming cultural conflict into creative friction through the integrating power of dialogue. Her current passion is the creation of "microcultures" for the development of new dynamics and connectivity between men and women. She lives in Frankfurt, Germany, and among too many other things, is working on two new book projects related to her work on gender and the evolution of culture.

For more, go to:
www.elizabethdebold.com

Tahil Sharma
Brave New Films

1. How do you define social harmony?

I define social harmony as more than just diversity. When we look at the history of civilization and the interactions of cultures, religions, and empires, we realize that diversity is inherent in the existence of humankind; we do not live on the same terms but recognize our social and cultural contexts may share a common thread. Not recognizing those commonalities and the thirst for conquest or self-righteousness creates greater enmity than the possibility of bridge-building.

This is why social harmony can only exist when we are in pursuit of pluralism. Pluralism is defined as an active engagement of diverse ideologies, backgrounds, and upbringings in an attempt to contextualize relationships and build stronger bridges between individuals and the communities they represent. In a society filled with social harmony, each individual recognizes their equality with another individual, in full regard to where they come from and how they got to this point in life. When they see each other as equals in some way, it becomes easier to speak with folks who you may have disagreements with, all while being able to leave the conversation on a positive note. When diversity is actively engaged in a productive way, from conversations to the responsibility of repairing a broken world together, you will have achieved the practice of pluralism. Ultimately, it is pluralism that creates social harmony because the goal is not equality (what we must consider innate and fundamental from the start) but equity, the pursuit of a just, impartial process for all to achieve their dreams as we create a better tomorrow. When we all share the opportunity to pursue stable lives, families, and futures for ourselves and each other, only then can we see a thorough and sustainable social harmony that we deserve in the world.

2. What is the best bridge-building technique you have come across or used?

The best bridge-building technique I have ever come across is contextual storytelling. For as long as our cultures and traditions can be traced, if not longer, we can tell that there have been traces of storytelling through writings and art that tell us about the development of our species. Storytelling in the 21st Century has been the balm of healing that has mended divisions and dissolved the vitriol that is exacerbated by hate and ignorance. The common lessons and empathy building that come from telling stories is the very reason that folks that seem like the most unlikely of friends become so when common experiences, struggles, and triumphs lead people to see themselves in others. I've used storytelling hundreds of times in lectures on interreligious literacy, to issues of human rights and social justice to make communities that may be privileged or unaware of the plights and injustices that may affect marginalized minority communities.

3. What does your organization do to promote social harmony?

Brave New Films works to use media platforms such as documentary films and shorter videos for social media to tell the stories of the people impacted by policies and injustices across the United States. My goal as the Program Manager for Brave New Faith Partners, helps to deliver the content of statistics, impact, and the human stories behind so many crises to communities of faith and moral conscience and create forums and discussion guides that make even the most difficult conversations of political and social issues palatable for religious communities and institutions. For the sake of promoting social harmony, it becomes the responsibility to the faithful and the moral to look past the veil of political competition and selfish agendas to see the moral urgency in tackling issues such as gun violence, climate change, food insecurity, and xenophobia. As we deliver the materials that help to raise awareness and educate communities about a variety of issues, it then becomes imperative for these newly inspired communities to engage in actions beyond the pews and pulpits; we hope that our films become the catalyst for community members to become more engaged in the political process through civic engagement and political accountability.

Biography

Tahil Sharma is a Southern California native born to a Hindu and Sikh Indian family. He is a nationally recognized leader promoting religious and secular pluralism, human rights, and social justice.

Tahil works as a Project Manager for Brave New Faith Partners as a part of Brave New Films, an organization that champions social justice issues by using a model of media, education, and grassroots volunteer involvement that inspires, empowers, motivates and teaches civic participation and makes a difference.

Tahil also serves as a Religious Director from the Office of Religious Life at the University of Southern California working on local initiatives to promote inter-religious dialogue and community engagement with students of diverse religious and secular backgrounds, with emphasis on South Asian and Hindu students, with support of the Germanacos Fellowship through the Interfaith Youth Core.

He also serves as an Los Angeles Coordinator for Sadhana: A Coalition of Progressive Hindus, a member of the NextGen Task Force for the Parliament of the World's Religions, and as a Youth Advisor to the Guibord Center in Los Angeles.

Recognized for his work in issues of social justice and interfaith cooperation, he was named a member of the Future50 cohort, a collaborative of the Interreligious Council of Southern California and USC's Center for Religion and Civic Culture that recognizes interfaith members within Southern California who will impact the landscape of religious diversity and service for the next half century.

Tahil was named a Newman Civic Fellow by Campus Compact for engaging diverse communities while working for food security in his local communities by building and maintaining garden beds that grow organic fruits and vegetables that are donated to food banks.

Linda Marks
MIFA (Metropolitan Inter-Faith Association)

1. How do you define social harmony?

It is illuminating to me to think of social harmony in the same terms as musical harmony. One kind of musical harmony is quite simple — for example when a soprano sings "Twinkle, Twinkle, Little Star," and an alto sings a third below the melody. The harmony created in this way is pleasing, at least to an ear conditioned to Western music, but it doesn't offer much nuance, texture, or vitality. This is the kind of harmony I think of when someone asks, "Why can't people just get along?" In music, it doesn't do much to allow for the unique qualities and potential of individual voices, and in life, it doesn't do much to allow for the rich diversity of human beings.

If you ask a 90-year-old from Cleveland, Ohio, what music sounds harmonic to her, the answer will differ greatly from the answer you'd get from a 25-year-old from Rangpur in Bangladesh. Just as musical harmony must encompass many different styles and tonalities, social harmony must encompass and invite many different ways that people relate to each other.

I can revel in a Beethoven symphony while

my friend in the concert hall across the street enjoys Gahu drumming from Ghana. As we each listen to music that pleases us, we are in harmony. The only thing that would ruin this harmony would be if the drummers across the street brought their instruments to my concert and played them during the Adagio of the Beethoven.

Social harmony, then, must embrace a world of differences between people and groups without imposing anyone on another or insisting that anyone is superior.

2. What is the best bridge-building technique you have come across or used?

In my experience, bridge-building is most effective and most sustainable when it happens gradually and in small steps. It is not shocking or unusual for us to have natural preferences for what we are accustomed to. Change, and embracing differences, requires us to stretch ourselves beyond what is comfortable, and it takes energy.

We can try to use our will to remove biases, but when we do this, we are dealing with abstractions, as when we say, "I must learn to be more comfortable with a person of a different race, faith, or sexual orientation." We're likely to fail with this approach. But taking small steps to be with and present to someone quite different leads to sustainable growth and openness. Simply sharing a brief conversation with a person we normally wouldn't encounter can start the process. The more we do it, the more we learn to be comfortable and confident in taking the next steps.

3. What does your organization do to promote social harmony?

My organization, MIFA (Metropolitan Inter-Faith Association) in Memphis, offers people the opportunity to take the first step beyond their comfort zone in a number of ways. Probably the most powerful is our Meals on Wheels program. A successful Jewish attorney from an upscale suburb might know the 92-year-old blind Baptist woman living alone in a run-down inner city area only as one of "the poor" until he starts delivering a meal to her every Thursday, hears her stories, sees her sparkle, and learns how she has survived and thrived. Maybe she will tell him about the dances she did when she was young and give him her recipe for biscuits. What might have begun from a sense of duty for him enlarges his world, and makes room for him to value people he previously might have merely felt sorry for or even feared.

Biography

Linda grew up in Memphis and is a graduate of Hutchison School. In 1967, she graduated from Agnes Scott College, in Decatur, GA, where she majored in English, accompanied the Glee Club, and was active in student government. She received her M.A. in English at the University of Wisconsin-Madison, and taught both high school and college English. In 1986, she received her J.D. from Cecil C. Humphreys School of Law at the University of Memphis, and became a patient rights advocate and conflict resolution specialist during her many years in Portland, ME. In 2004, she returned to Memphis and began working at the Metropolitan Inter-Faith Association (MIFA), an organization founded in 1968 after Dr. King's assassination for the purpose of helping to heal the community. Her position as MIFA's Inter-Faith and Community Outreach Officer has given her the opportunity both to appreciate the distinctiveness of many faith traditions and to bring diverse groups together to support MIFA's vision of uniting the community through service. Linda is a musician and throughout her life has accompanied choruses, soloists, choirs, and community theater productions.

Rev. Stephen Kinney
The Front Porch Project

1. How do you define social harmony?

I define it in terms of my understanding of the problem of *"the one and the many."* The pre-Socratic Greek philosophers posed this as the tension between Parmenides (the one) and Heraclitus (the many). Early Christian philosophers reconciled this tension through their grasp of "the Trinity", i.e., the triadic dynamic/relationship at the heart of the cosmos, whereby the binary oppositions between the one (always in danger of collapsing into a totalizing, centripetal One) and the many (always in danger of centrifugal chaos) were neutralized and reconciled by a "third." The "Trinity", then, sought to name the reality that social harmony was ontological—i.e., unique and differentiated persons share oneness/communion without merging into a bland unity that overrides their uniqueness or erased their distinctions. In fact, their union is constituted by and dependent upon each other. They thus exist in social harmony. So that's how I define it: a co-constitutive interpenetrating harmony that reveals the personhood of each constituent.

2. What is the best bridge-building technique you have come across or used?

I have found that bringing people together through music or art (perhaps this functions as that "third thing"?) provides a way to transcend the usual oppositions to community. That is, by directing our attention to something beautiful outside of ourselves enables us to forget ourselves long enough to let "the other" in. Overcoming self-consciousness opens us to broader/deeper horizons. "Ground Rules" are helpful here: I extend the invitation to recognize that when we welcome the other (hospitality), we may discover that our differences may be enriching rather than threatening.

We use the metaphor of "The Front Porch" to invite people to gather together in non-instrumental ways to pay attention and become aware of the gifts around and between us. It's an attitude for opening the heart to the other (a.k.a., humility) that promotes suspending our own limited perspectives long enough to be penetrated by the presence and ideas of others. Social interpenetration, as such, leads to learning new things and to co-creating and partnering with others. It's a way for expanding our horizons.

3. What does your organization do to promote social harmony?

We provide opportunities and excuses for gathering together through music, art, special events, etc. We do so with an intentionality to share communion with different "others." We do so with the expectation and confidence that something new always emerges between us when we suspend our own beliefs in order to learn from others. Our own 'beliefs' are thereby enriched and enlarged. When this happens, there is fun and excitement.

Biography

Stephen Kinney is an Episcopal priest in the Diocese of Texas and currently serves as the Director of The Front Porch Project, which is a mission of All Saints' Episcopal Church in Austin. The Front Porch brings people together from all over Austin through a weekly "public-house church," music and cultural events, and dialogue. After serving as a youth minister, chaplain, and rector in schools and parishes in Houston, New York City, and Fredericksburg, he and his family moved to Austin, where he earned a Ph.D. in Educational Psychology with a focus on dialogical relationships (dissertation: Sustaining Marriage in a Post-Traditional, Postmodern World), led a family service at St. David's Episcopal Church, taught at the Seminary of the Southwest and UT as an adjunct faculty. Stephen is currently the President of Interfaith Action Central Texas (iACT). He is married to Gwen, a licensed therapist, and father of Matthew, Kathleen, and Tyler. Apart from drinking beer and coffee in pubs and cafes, Stephen likes to catch fish and grow vegetables. B.A., University of Texas; M.Div., Episcopal Seminary of the Southwest; M.A., University of Texas; Ph.D., University of Texas.

RESOURCES

The following list of resources can aid in your work towards co-human harmony. It includes a list of organizations, TED talks, YouTube videos, and books. We will continue to add to this list on our website, *www.harmonyii.org*, and welcome ideas and submissions.

Organizations

- NAIN (North American Interfaith Network)
  www.nain.org
- Parliament of the World's Religions
  www.parliamentofreligions.org
- URI (United Religions Initiative)
  www.uri.org
- Charter for Compassion
  www.charterforcompassion.org

- Convergence on Campus
  www.convergenceoncampus.org
- Interfaith Youth Core
  www.ifyc.org
- Dialogue that Depolarizes
  www.buildingpeacebypeace.org
- Dignity Dialogues
  www.dignitydialogues.com
- Compassion Course
  www.compassioncourse.org
- Compassion Summit
  www.compassionsummit.org
- MIFA (Metropolitan Inter-Faith Association)
  www.mifa.org
- Religions for Peace
  www.religionsforpeace.org
- Dialogue Institute Austin
  www.thedialoginstitute.org/austin/
- Men's Fellowship Network
  www.mensfellowship.net
- Tanenbaum
  www.tanenbaum.org
- One World in Dialogue
  www.oneworldindialogue.com
- Goldin Institute
  www.goldininstitute.org
- World Faith Development Dialogue
  www.berkleycenter.georgetown.edu/wfdd
- Compassionate Listening
  www.compassionatelistening.org
- iACT (Interfaith Action of Central Texas)
  www.interfaithtexas.org

- Interfaith Alliance
  www.interfaithalliance.org
- Alliance for Peacebuilding
  www.allianceforpeacebuilding.org
- National Coalition for Dialogue and Deliberation
  www.ncdd.org
- Center for Interfaith Relations
  www.centerforinterfaithrelations.org
- Interfaith Encounter Association
  www.interfaith-encounter.org
- The Elijah Interfaith Institute
  www.elijah-interfaith.org
- The Interfaith Observer (media)
  www.theinterfaithobserver.org
- The Pluralism Project
  www.pluralism.org
- Kaufman Interfaith Institute
  www.gvsu.edu/interfaith
- More in Common
  www.moreincommon.com
- Scarboro Missions
  www.scarboromissions.ca
- Interfaith Amigos
  www.interfaithamigos.com

TED talks

www.ted.com

- Megan Phelps-Roper: I grew up in the Westboro Baptist Church. Here's why I left.
- Karen Armstrong: My wish - The Charter for Compassion

- Jonathan Haidt: The moral roots of liberals and conservatives
- Amy Edmondson: How to turn a group of strangers into a team
- Azim Khamisa and Ples Felix: What comes after tragedy? Forgiveness
- Nabila Alibhai: Why people of different faiths are painting their houses of worship yellow
- Chelsea Shields: How I'm working for change inside my church
- Rabbi Lord Jonathan Sacks: How we can face the future without fear, together
- Erez Yoeli: How to motivate people to do good for others

YouTube Videos

www.youtube.com

- The Interfaith Amigos: Breaking the taboos of interfaith dialogue
  https://youtu.be/tPnZArtsG_c
- Betty Williams: Shameless Idealists
  https://youtu.be/OIJFNpPqj-w
- Padraig O'Malley: The Peacemaker Q&A
  https://youtu.be/9CKsEw25B8g
- Yehuda Stolov: 12 Faces of Hope
  https://youtu.be/qJXoLgN9L4k
- Dirk Ficca: Interview
  https://youtu.be/vg9_g_fbwl4
- Mehnaz Afridi: Interview
  https://youtu.be/vMFd28zIj_4
- Daniel Kahneman: Thinking Fast vs. Thinking Slow

https://youtu.be/PirFrDVRBo4
- Eboo Patel: To narrow toxic divides, students build bridges between faiths *https://youtu.be/7JGNPX3b5LQ*

Books

- *Experifaith: At the Heart of Every Religion-* Gudjon Bergmann
- *The World's Religions* - Huston Smith
- *The Righteous Mind* - Jonathan Haidt
- *Thinking Fast and Slow* - Daniel Kahneman
- *Twelve Steps to a Compassionate Life* - Karen Armstrong
- *How Can I Help* - Paul Gorman and Ram Dass
- *Non-Violent Resistance (Satyagraha)* - Mohandas K. Gandhi
- *Long Walk to Freedom* - Nelson Mandela
- *Out of Many Faiths* - Eboo Patel
- *Thank you for Arguing* - Jay Heinrichs
- *Changing Minds* - Howard Gardner
- *Influence* - Robert Cialdini
- *Rising Out of Hatred* - Eli Saslow
- *Religious Literacy* - Stephen Prothero
- *Strength to Love* - Martin Luther King. Jr.

ABOUT THE AUTHOR AND THE ORGANIZATION

The Author

Born in Iceland in 1972, Rev. Gudjon Bergmann moved to the USA in 2010 and became a U.S. citizen in 2013. He is an ordained Interfaith Minister, the founder and lead educator at Harmony Interfaith Initiative, a devoted husband, and proud father of two.

Rev. Bergmann has written over twenty books, both fiction and nonfiction. His two novels are spiritual but not mindlessly positive, mysterious but don't revolve around criminal elements, and philosophical but not so deep as to put the reader to sleep. His nonfiction books are practical and to the point. He has written extensively about self-development and spirituality, including books on yoga, meditation, smoking cessation, stress management, interfaith and more.

The Organization

Gudjon and Johanna Bergmann founded Harmony Interfaith Initiative in February 2018, an educational and social good organization that envisions a world where people have good access to strategies, methods, and ideas that promote social harmony and enable bridge-building across divides. Offerings include programs, workshops, consultation services, talks, partnerships, and more.

Organizational Values

- *Progress Over Perfection*: Bridges are built brick by brick and social harmony exists on a spectrum from ceasing hostilities to compassionate fellowship. We value progress over perfection. All our programs reflect that sentiment.
- *Simple But Never Shallow*: Universal ideas are simple, but they also allow for depth. We believe in presenting our programs with clarity for a broad audience while simultaneously allowing for enough depth to satisfy academics and deep thinkers.
- *Strategies Over Platitudes*: If it were enough to tell people to "be friends" and "be nice to each other" then there would be no acrimony or division in the world. We know from experience that people need practical ideas, strategies, and methods that can be applied.

- *Practice and Maintenance*: Continual practice is essential for progress. Without practice, the ideas and strategies we present are easily reduced to wishful thinking. Furthermore, since all good things can deteriorate, it is important to set a maintenance schedule once a good habit has been formed.

- *We Are Always Learning and Growing*: We have gathered some of the best ideas and practices for bridge-building and social harmony… but we don't know everything. We are continually reading, learning, exploring, improving, and growing. And we're always open to feedback and suggestions.

- *All-Inclusive Definition of Faith*: As an interfaith organization, we define faith as, *complete trust, confidence or strong belief in someone or something.* This means that our definition includes all belief systems, both religious and secular in nature. We believe in building bridges between all those who share strong opposite beliefs.

- *Harmony Over Uniformity*: Diversity is baked into the cake at this point. All we can do is decide what to do about it. We know that the world is a better place when people of different backgrounds, ideas, and beliefs attempt to live together in harmony.

To learn more, visit *www.harmonyii.org*

Made in the USA
Las Vegas, NV
11 August 2023